SCHOLASTIC

LITTLE LEARNER PACKETS

WORD FAMILIES

Violet Findley

Cover design: Tannaz Fassihi; Cover illustration: Jason Dove
Interior design: Michelle H. Kim
Interior illustration: Doug Jones

ISBN: 978-1-338-23030-7

Printed in the U.S.A.
First printing, January 2018.

2 3 4 5 6 7 8 9 10 40 24 23 22 21 20 19

Table of Contents

Introduction

Looking for a playful way to help children recognize and read the top spelling patterns in print? Welcome to *Little Learner Packets: Word Families*! The 10 reproducible learning packets in this book provide targeted practice with 20 essential phonograms—otherwise known as *word families*—to set the stage for early reading success.

Each packet invites children to read, trace, write, match, find, graph, and gain lots of experience with two target word families. You can use the learning packets in a variety of ways and with children of all learning styles. Children can complete the activities at their seats or in a learning center. Or they can use the pages as take-home practice.

The packets are ideal for encouraging children to work independently and at their own pace. A grid on the introduction page of each packet lets children track their progress as they complete each page. Best of all, the activities support children in meeting must-know literacy standards for kindergarten, first, and second grade. (See the Connections to the Standards box.)

Happy learning!

Connections to the Standards

Print Concepts
Demonstrate understanding of the organization and basic features of print.

Phonological Awareness
Demonstrate understanding of spoken words, syllables, and sounds.

Phonics and Word Recognition
Know and apply grade-level phonics and word analysis skills in decoding words.

Phonics Packets

PACKET 1: –an, –at

PACKET 2: –ed, –ell

PACKET 3: –ick, –ing

PACKET 4: –ot, –ock

PACKET 5: –ug, –uck

PACKET 6: –am, –ap

PACKET 7: –ill, –ip

PACKET 8: –ail, –ake

PACKET 9: –ee, –eep

PACKET 10: –ice, –ight

How to Use the Word Families Packets

Copy a class supply of the eight pages for the word families packet you want to use. Then sequence and staple each set of pages together and distribute the packets to children. All they need to complete the pages are pencils and crayons. TIP: To conserve paper, simply make double-sided copies.

The format of the learning packets makes the pages easy to use. Here's what you'll find on each page:

Page 1 / Introduction: This page introduces the packet's two target word families, such as *–an* and *–at*. Children fill in the missing phonograms to create six new words. When the activity is finished, children check off the first box in the tracking grid at the bottom. As they complete each of the remaining pages in the packet, children will check off the corresponding box in the grid.

Pages 2 & 5 / Read & Write: Children read the illustrated "story sentence" featuring words in the target word family. They then write the those words several times to boost awareness of that phonogram and build handwriting skills. The bottom of the page includes a bonus activity that challenges children to create three new words in the word family.

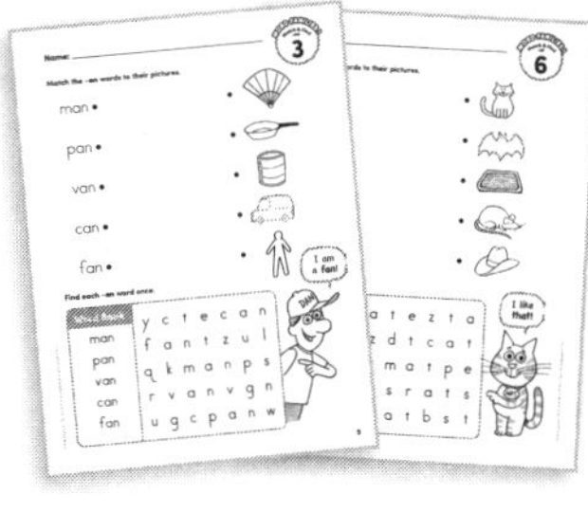

Pages 3 & 6 / Match & Find: At the top of the page, children reinforce discrimination skills by matching target words to their pictures. At the bottom of the page, children locate each word in a simple hidden-word puzzle. NOTE: Each word-family word appears in the puzzle once horizontally.

Pages 4 & 7 / Graph: The fun graphing activity gives children the opportunity to reinforce phonogram knowledge and counting skills simultaneously. TIP: Extend math learning by inviting children to explore and discuss the graph's results.

Page 8 / Review: Children complete a humorous, illustrated story by writing six target word-family words in the appropriate blanks. TIP: When the blanks are filled in, boost early literacy skills by running your finger under the text and reading the story aloud together.

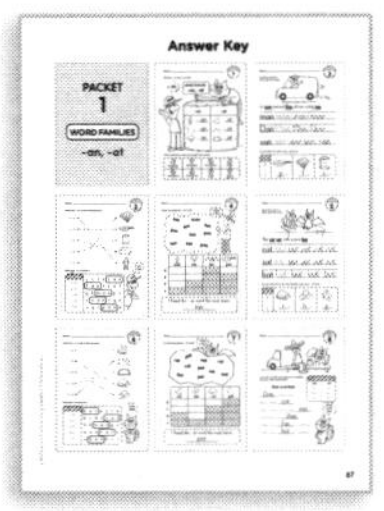

Answer Key: A handy answer key is provided on pages 87–96. The thumbnail images allow you to check children's completed pages at a glance. You can then use the results to determine areas in which they might need additional instruction or practice.

Teaching Tips

Use these tips to help children get the most from the learning packets.

- ★ **Provide a model:** Demonstrate, step by step, how to complete each page in the first packet. Children should then be able to complete the remaining packets independently.
- ★ **Focus on the target words:** Have children identify each word-family word and finger-write it in the air. You can also work together to craft simple sentences that include those target words. After they're written, read them aloud together!
- ★ **Offer Additional Practice:** Read word-family lists. Play word-family games. Listen to word-family songs. Write word-family stories. And, of course, read, read, read!

Learning Centers

You might label a separate folder with each child's name and place the packets in the folder to keep in a learning center. Then children can retrieve the assigned packet and work independently through the pages during center time. To make the packets self-checking, you can enlarge the answer keys for each packet, cut apart the images, then sequence and staple them together to create a mini answer key for that packet. Finally, place all of the answer keys in the center. Children can refer to the answer key that corresponds to the packet they are working on to check their completed pages.

Ways to Use the Word Families Learning Packets

Children can work through the packets at their own pace, tracking their progress as they complete each page. The packets are ideal for the following:

- ★ Learning center activity
- ★ Independent seatwork
- ★ One-on-one lesson
- ★ Morning starter
- ★ End of the day wrap-up
- ★ Take-home practice

Assessing Learning

To quickly assess children's word-family skills, do the following:

- ★ Display words with each target word family and have children read them aloud.
- ★ Call out words in each target word family and have children write them down.
- ★ Call out a target phonogram and have children respond with words in the word family. TIP: Younger children can say the words. Older children can write the words.

Name: ____

WORD FAMILIES 1
Introduction
1

Fill in the -**an** and -**at** words.

Color in each box when you complete an activity.

① Introduction -an & -at	② Read & Write -an	③ Match & Find -an	④ Graph -an
⑤ Read & Write -at	⑥ Match & Find -at	⑦ Graph -at	⑧ Review -an & -at

Name: ______________________________

Read the sentence.
Then write the words.

A **man** named **Dan** drives a big **van**.

man man

Dan Dan

van van

Use the letters to make more -**an** words.

Letter Bank			
p c f	______an	______an	______an

Name: ____

Match the -**an** words to their pictures.

man •

pan •

van •

can •

fan •

Find each -**an** word once.

Word Bank							
man	y	c	t	e	c	a	n
pan	f	a	n	t	z	u	l
van	q	k	m	a	n	p	s
can	r	v	a	n	v	g	n
fan	u	g	c	p	a	n	w

Name: ______________________________

Count and graph the **-an** words.

Math is fun!

tan man
fan tan
pan
tan pan
tan fan pan

DAN

	 man	 fan	 tan	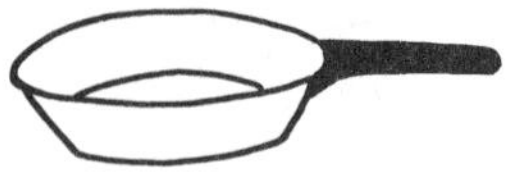 pan
4				
3				
2				
1				

I found this –an word the most times:

____

Name: ____________________

Read the sentence.
Then write the words.

The **cat** **sat** with a nice **bat**.

cat cat

sat sat

bat bat

Use the letters from the letter bank to make more -at words.

Letter Bank			
p r h	____at	____at	____at

Name: ______________________________

WORD FAMILIES 1 Match & Find -at 6

Match the -**at** words to their pictures.

cat •	•	
rat •	•	
hat •	•	
mat •	•	
bat •	•	

Find each -**at** word once.

Word Bank							
cat	h	a	t	e	z	t	a
hat	b	z	d	t	c	a	t
mat	h	k	m	a	t	p	e
bat	w	a	s	r	a	t	s
rat	u	b	a	t	b	s	t

Name: ______________________________

WORD FAMILIES! Graph -at 7

Count and graph the **-at** words.

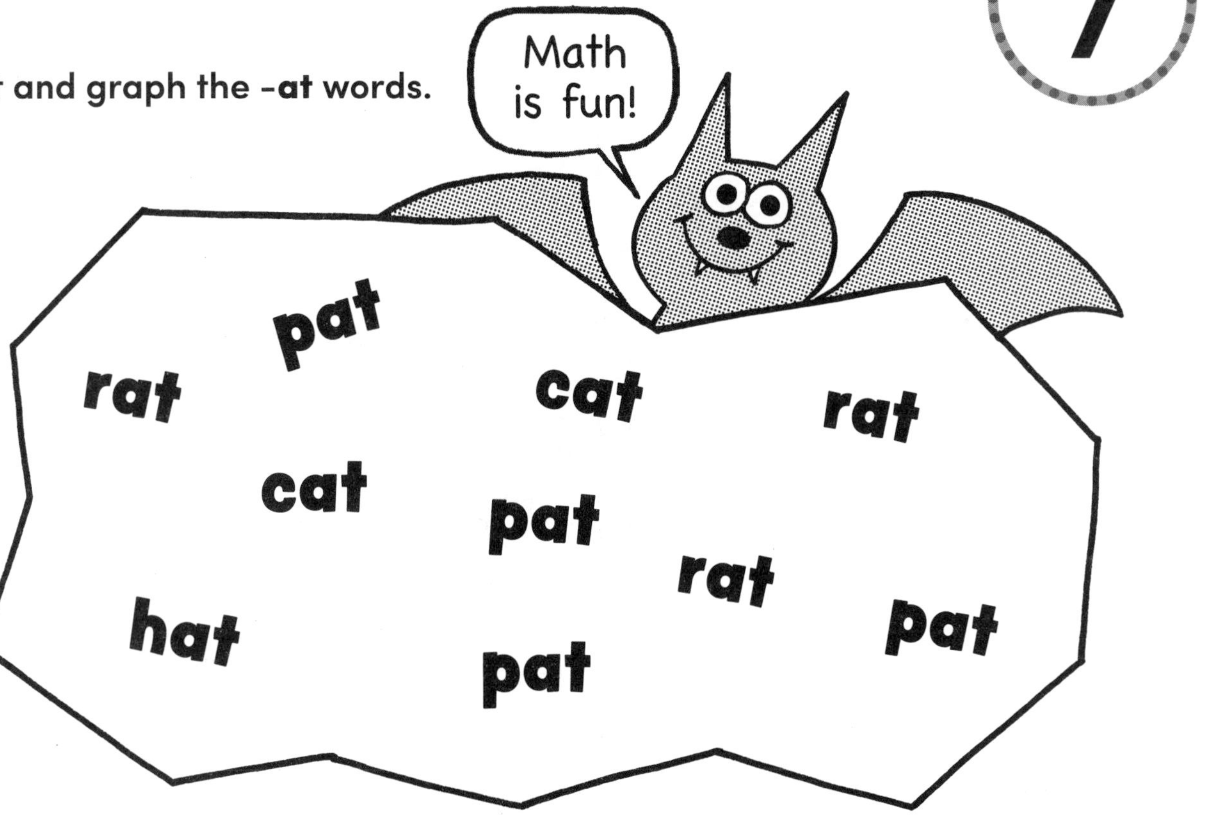

Math is fun!

pat rat cat rat cat pat rat hat pat pat

	 cat	 hat	 rat	 pat
4				
3				
2				
1				

I found this –at word the most times:

____

Name: ______________________________

Use each -an and -at word once to complete the story. Then read it aloud.

Word Bank	
-an	**-at**
fan	cat
Dan	hat
van	chat

Dan and Nat

__________ is that man.

Nat is that __________.

They sat by a big, tan __________

and had a nice__________.

"I like your __________!" said Dan.

"I like your __________!" said Nat.

Name: ____________________________________

Fill in the **-ed** and **-ell** words.

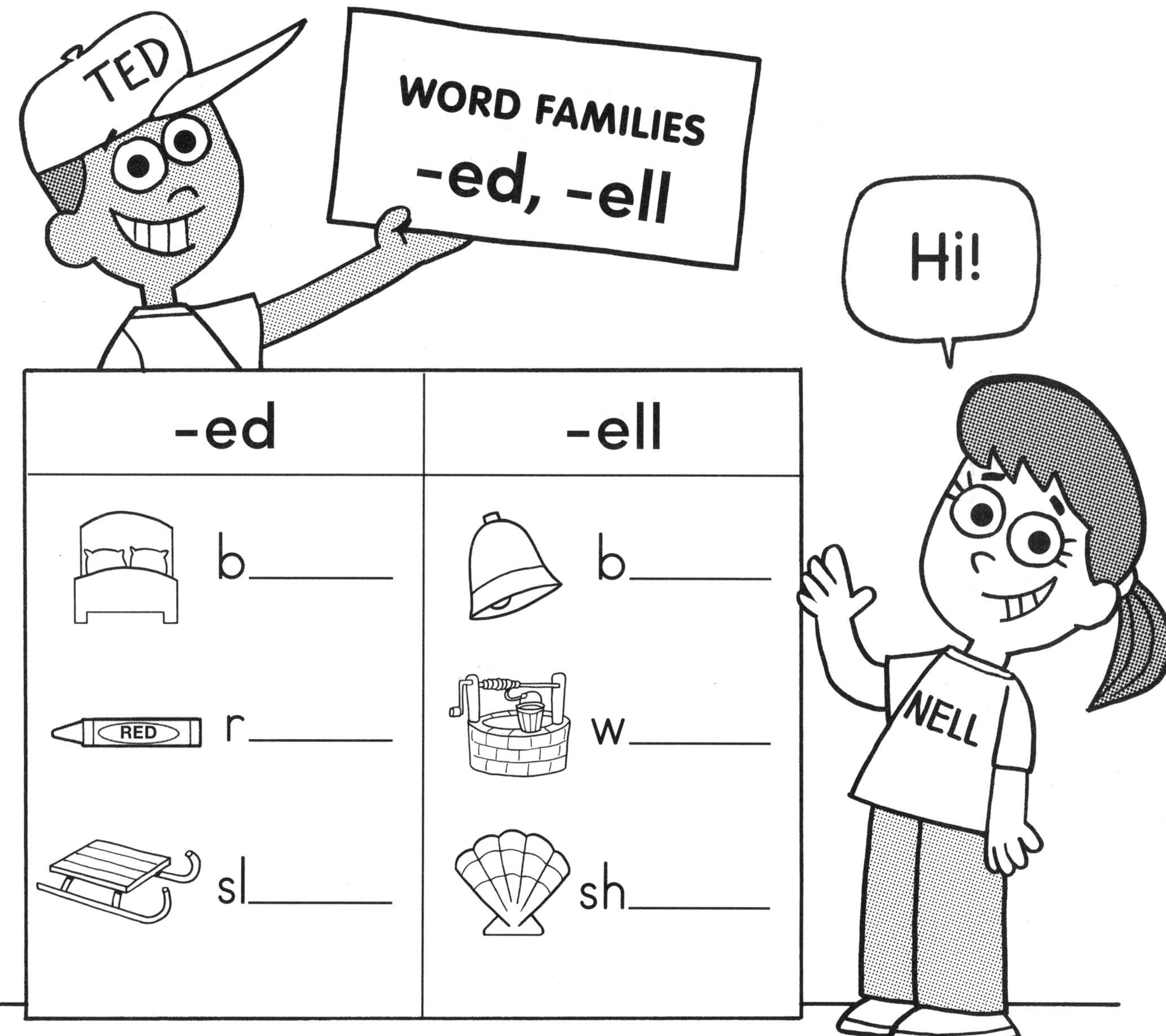

-ed	-ell
b_____	b_____
r_____	w_____
sl_____	sh_____

Color in each box when you complete an activity.

1 Introduction -ed & -ell	2 Read & Write -ed	3 Match & Find -ed	4 Graph -ed
5 Read & Write -ell	6 Match & Find -ell	7 Graph -ell	8 Review -ed & -ell

Name: ____________________

WORD FAMILIES 2
Read & Write -ed
2

Read the sentence.
Then write the words.

TED
RED

A boy named **Ted** paints his **sled** **red**.

Ted Ted

sled sled

red red

Use the letters from the letter bank to make more -**ed** words.

Name: ____________________

WORD FAMILIES 2
Match & Find -ed
3

Match the **-ed** words to their pictures.

red • • 

bed • • 

sled • • 

wed • • 

shed • • 

Find each **-ed** word once.

Word Bank							
red	d	c	s	l	e	d	x
bed	r	e	d	t	z	u	v
sled	k	w	e	d	f	p	s
wed	e	a	s	b	e	d	l
shed	j	s	h	e	d	g	c

Name: ______________________________

Count and graph the -ed words.

Math is fun!

TED

sled

red

bed

wed

red

wed

sled

red

wed

red

	sled	red	bed	wed
4				
3				
2				
1				

I found this -ed word the most times:

____

Name: ______________________________

Read the sentence.
Then write the words.

A girl named **Nell** has a **shell** and a **bell**.

Nell Nell

shell shell

bell bell

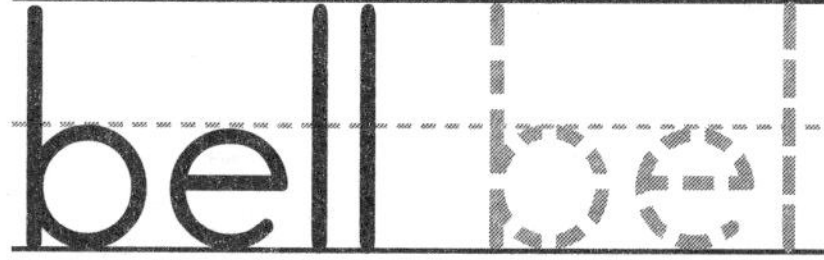

Use the letters from the letter bank to make more -ell words.

Letter Bank			
y sm w	______ell	______ell	______ell

WORD FAMILIES 2
Match & Find
-ell
6

Name: ______________________________

Match the **-ell** words to their pictures.

smell • 

shell •

yell •

bell •

well •

Find each **-ell** word once.

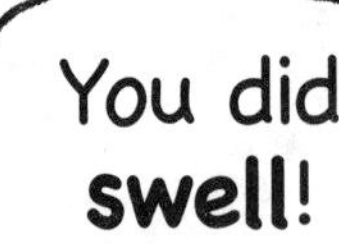

Word Bank							
bell	w	e	l	l	n	t	e
shell	z	b	e	l	l	u	v
yell	q	k	o	y	e	l	l
smell	s	h	e	l	l	g	n
well	u	g	s	m	e	l	l

Name: ______________________________

Count and graph the -ell words.

Math is fun!

sell shell sell smell shell bell shell bell sell shell

NELL

	bell	smell	shell	sell
4				
3				
2				
1				

I found this –ell word the most times:

____

Name: ____________________

Use each -ed and -ell word once to complete the story. Then read it aloud.

Word Bank	
-ed	**-ell**
shed	bell
Ted	Nell
sled	shell

Ted and Nell

His name is __________.

He has a red __________.

Her name is __________.

She has a sea __________

and a big __________.

Where will they keep their stuff?

Inside the __________!

Name: ____________________

WORD FAMILIES 3
Introduction
1

Fill in the **-ick** and **-ing** words.

Color in each box when you complete an activity.

1 Introduction -ick & -ing	2 Read & Write -ick	3 Match & Find -ick	4 Graph -ick
5 Read & Write -ing	6 Match & Find -ing	7 Graph -ing	8 Review -ick & -ing

Name: ______________________________

Read the sentence.
Then write the words.

"I love to **lick** my lollipop!"
said a **chick** named **Nick**.

lick lick

chick chick

Nick Nick

Use the letters from the letter bank to make more -ick words.

Letter Bank			
tr k st	______ick	______ick	______ick

WORD FAMILIES 3
Match & Find
-ick
3

Name: ______________________________

Match the -**ick** words to their pictures.

chick •   • 

stick •   • 

kick •   • 

brick •   • 

sick •   • 

Find each -**ick** word once.

Word Bank							
sick	c	a	k	i	c	k	v
stick	b	z	c	h	i	c	k
chick	s	i	c	k	f	p	e
kick	r	s	t	i	c	k	n
brick	u	g	b	r	i	c	k

Name: ______________________________

Count and graph the -**ick** words.

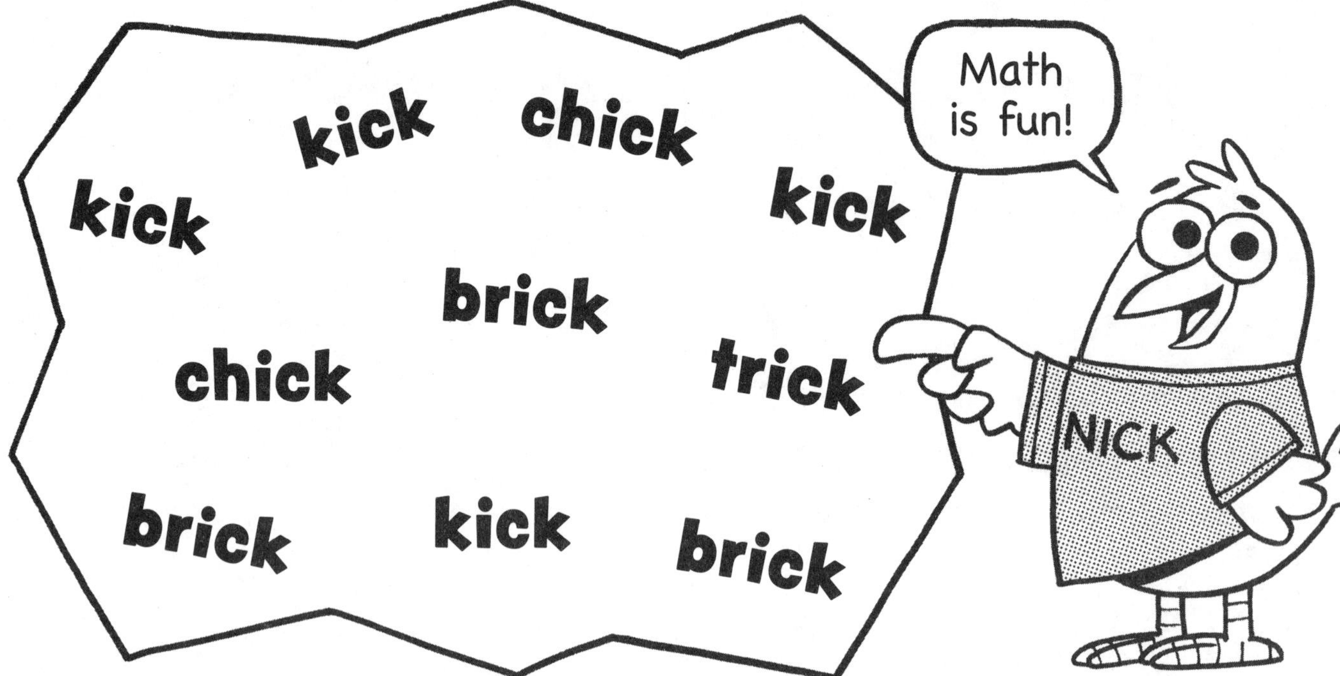

	chick	kick	brick	trick
4				
3				
2				
1				

I found this -ick word the most times:

____

Name: ______________________________

Read the sentence.
Then write the words.

The **king** loves to **swing** in the **spring**.

king king

swing swing

spring spring

Use the letters from the letter bank to make more **-ing** words.

Letter Bank			
r			
str			
w	____ing	____ing	____ing

Name: ______________________________

WORD FAMILIES 3
Match & Find -ing
6

Match the **-ing** words to their pictures.

king •	• 
ring •	• 
wing •	• 
sing •	• 
string •	• 

Find each **-ing** word once.

Word Bank							
king	s	c	w	i	n	g	a
ring	s	t	r	i	n	g	n
wing	q	k	o	s	i	n	g
sing	r	k	i	n	g	f	n
string	r	i	n	g	b	o	t

WORD FAMILIES 3
Graph -ing
7

Name: ______________________________

Count and graph the **-ing** words.

Math is fun!

wing king
wing sling wing
swing king
king swing
wing

	king	swing	wing	sling
4				
3				
2				
1				

I found this –ing word the most times:

____

Name: ________________________________

Use each -ick and -ing word once to complete the story. Then read it aloud.

Word Bank	
-ick	**-ing**
pick	swing
Nick	ring
chick	spring

The Chick and the King

Zick, zing!

The season is __________!

The king wears a __________.

The __________ has a lollipop.

His name is __________.

"I will __________ flowers," said the king.

"I will __________," said the chick.

Name: ______________________________

Fill in the **-ot** and **-ock** words.

-ot	-ock
d_____	 cl_____
 p_____	 s_____
 t_____	 bl_____

Color in each box when you complete an activity.

1 Introduction -ot & -ock	2 Read & Write -ot	3 Match & Find -ot	4 Graph -ot
5 Read & Write -ock	6 Match & Find -ock	7 Graph -ock	8 Review -ot & -ock

Name: ____________________

Read the sentence.
Then write the words.

Dot has a **pot** of **hot** spaghetti.

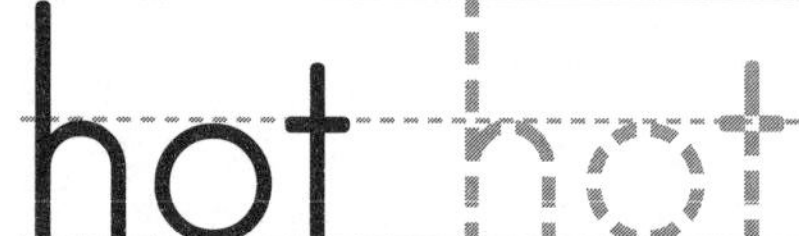

pot pot

hot hot

Use the letters from the letter bank to make more **-ot** words.

Letter Bank			
c sp kn	______ot	______ot	______ot

Name: ______________________________

Match the **-ot** words to their pictures.

pot •	•	
hot •	•	
tot •	•	
cot •	•	
spot •	•	

Find each **-ot** word once.

Word Bank							
pot	g	c	c	o	t	t	e
hot	t	o	t	t	z	u	p
tot	j	m	s	p	o	t	e
cot	g	h	o	t	g	j	o
spot	k	g	v	p	o	t	x

WORD FAMILIES 4
Graph -ot
4

Name: ______________________________

Count and graph the **-ot** words.

spot spot knot
pot knot
tot tot
knot spot knot

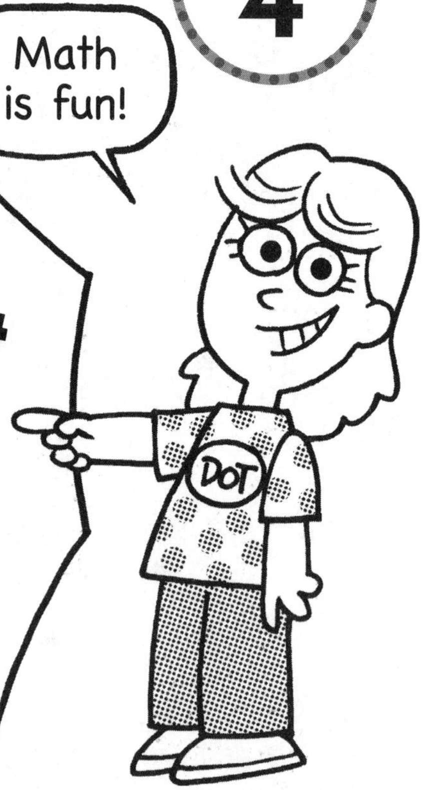

	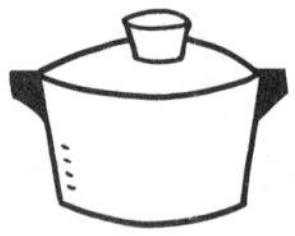 pot	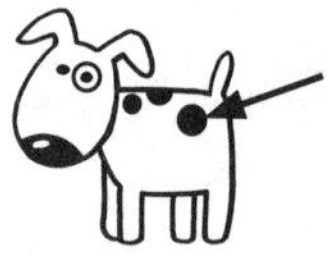 spot	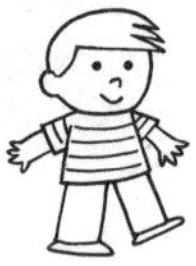 tot	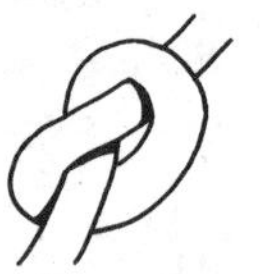 knot
4				
3				
2				
1				

I found this –ot word the most times:

____

Name: ______________________________

Read the sentence.
Then write the words.

The **clock** on the **rock** says, "Tick, **tock**."

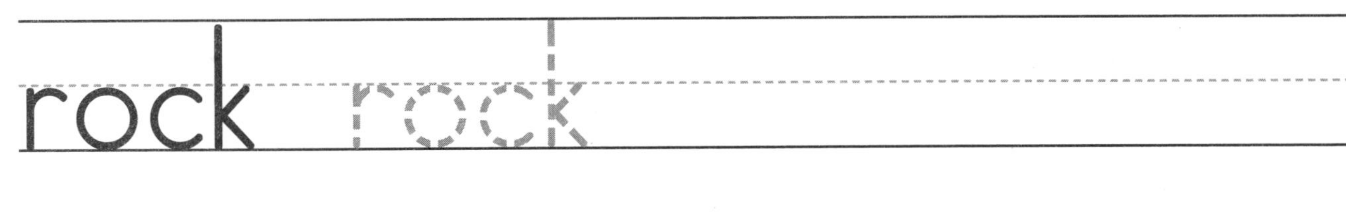

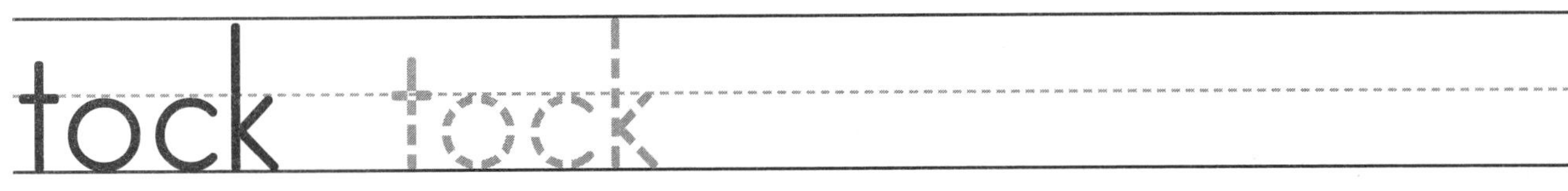

tock tock

Use the letters from the letter bank to make more -**ock** words.

Letter Bank			
s kn bl	_____ock	_____ock	_____ock

Name: ______________________________

Match the -**ock** words to their pictures.

clock •	• 
rock •	• 
sock •	• 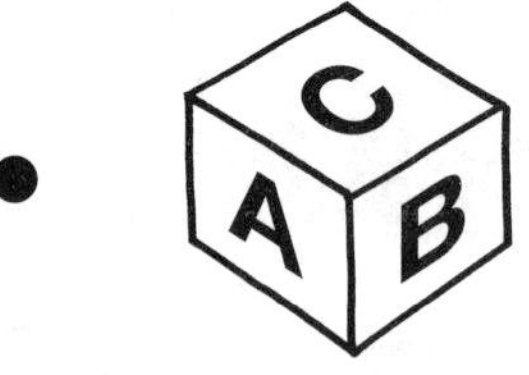
block •	• 
lock •	• 

Find each -**ock** word once.

Word Bank							
lock	s	c	t	r	o	c	k
clock	r	b	l	o	c	k	m
sock	f	k	o	l	o	c	k
block	c	l	o	c	k	g	n
rock	u	s	o	c	k	s	t

Name: ______________________________

Count and graph the -**ock** words.

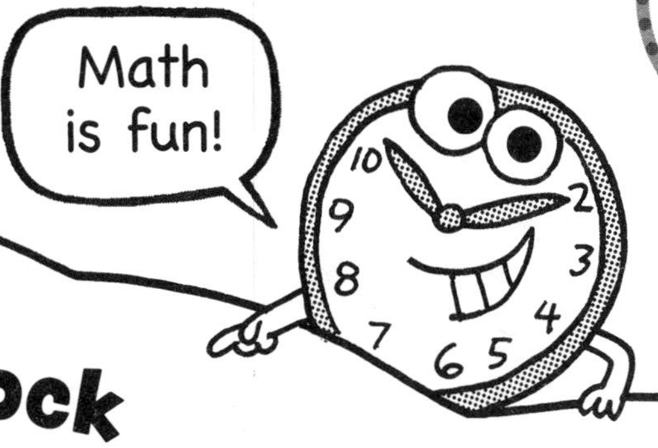

Math is fun!

dock rock

rock lock dock clock

rock

lock dock rock

	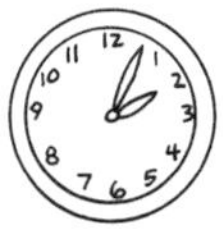 clock	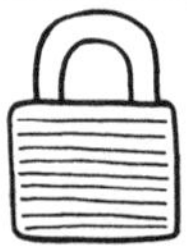 lock	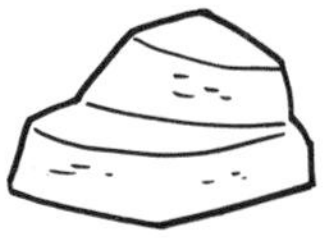 rock	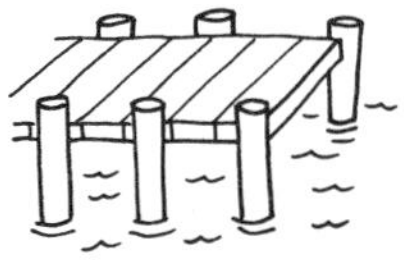 dock
4				
3				
2				
1				

I found this -ock word the most times:

____

Name: ____

Use each -ot and -ock word once to complete the story. Then read it aloud.

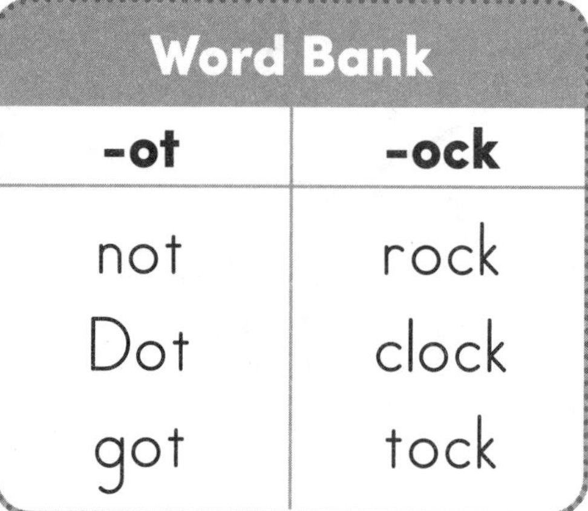

Word Bank	
-ot	**-ock**
not	rock
Dot	clock
got	tock

Dot and the Clock

__________ has a problem.

She does __________ like to wake up.

So she __________ a new clock.

At night, the clock says, "Tick, __________."

But in the morning, it says, "RING, RING!"

Hooray! The __________ wakes her up.

"Clock, you __________!" says Dot.

Name: ______________________________

Fill in the **-ug** and **-uck** words.

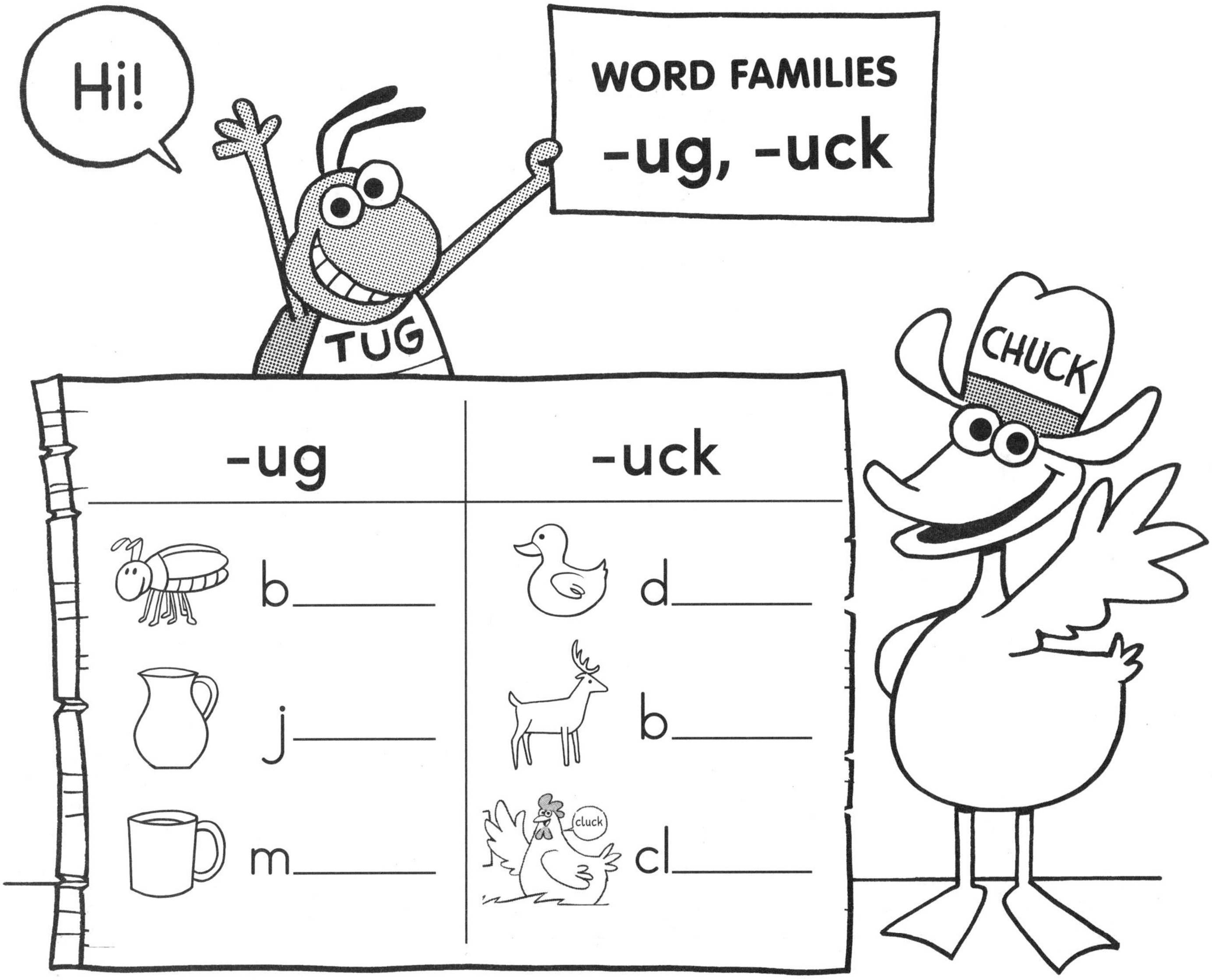

-ug	-uck
b_____	d_____
j_____	b_____
m_____	cl_____

Color in each box when you complete an activity.

1 Introduction -ug & -uck	2 Read & Write -ug	3 Match & Find -ug	4 Graph -ug
5 Read & Write -uck	6 Match & Find -uck	7 Graph -uck	8 Review -ug & -uck

Name: ______________________________

Read the sentence.
Then write the words.

A **bug** named **Tug** is in a **mug**.

bug bug

Tug Tug

mug mug

Use the letters from the letter bank to make more **-ug** words.

Letter Bank			
j pl r	____ug	____ug	____ug

WORD FAMILIES 5
Match & Find -ug
3

Name: ______________________________

Match the -**ug** words to their pictures.

jug •	•
rug •	• 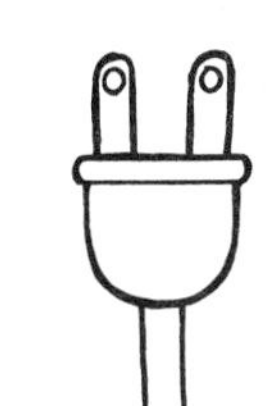
plug •	• 
slug •	• 
mug •	• 

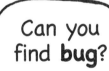

Find each -**ug** word once.

Can you find **bug**?

Word Bank							
slug	p	l	u	g	l	u	l
mug	b	e	s	l	u	g	m
bug	q	k	o	p	r	u	g
rug	b	u	g	e	x	u	z
plug	u	j	s	m	u	g	h

Name: ____________________

Count and graph the **-ug** words.

	bug	mug	rug	pug
4				
3				
2				
1				

I found this –ug word the most times:

____

Name: ______________________________

Read the sentence.
Then write the words.

A **duck** named **Chuck** is in a **truck**!

duck duck

Chuck Chuck

truck truck

Use the letters from the letter bank to make more -**uck** words.

Letter Bank			
tr b cl	(cluck) ______uck	______uck	______uck

Name: ___________________________

WORD FAMILIES 5
Match & Find -uck
6

Match the -**uck** words to their pictures.

duck • • 

truck • • 

buck • • 

luck • • 

stuck • • 

Find each -**uck** word once.

Word Bank							
buck	y	c	t	b	u	c	k
stuck	l	u	c	k	z	u	m
truck	d	u	c	k	f	p	e
duck	r	a	s	t	u	c	k
luck	t	r	u	c	k	s	t

WORD FAMILIES 5
Graph -uck
7

Name: ______________________________

Count and graph the **-uck** words.

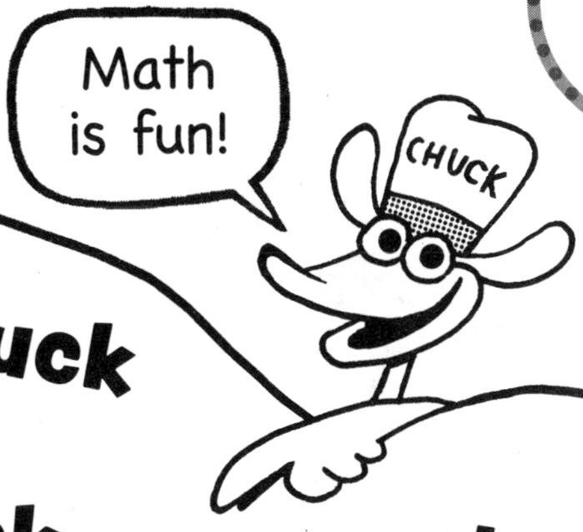
Math is fun!
CHUCK

truck **luck**

truck

cluck **duck**

duck **duck**

duck **truck** **luck**

	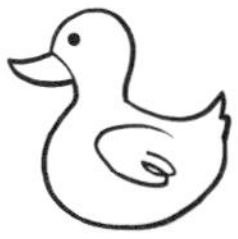 **duck**	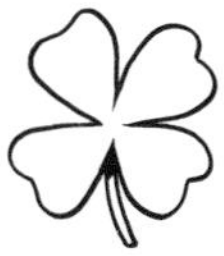 **luck**	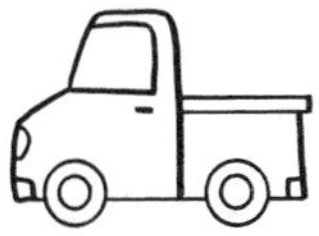 **truck**	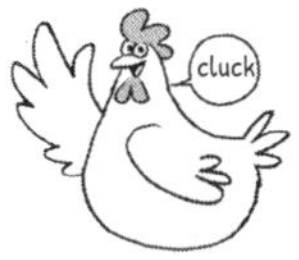 cluck **cluck**
4				
3				
2				
1				

I found this -uck word the most times:

____

Name: ____

Use each -ug and -uck word once to complete the story. Then read it aloud.

Word Bank	
-ug	**-uck**
mug	duck
jug	Chuck
bug	truck

Tug and Chuck

Tug is a __________.

Chuck is a __________.

Chuck drove his __________

over to see Tug.

Did __________ find Tug

in the __________? No!

Tug was in the __________!

Name: ________________________________

WORD FAMILIES 6
Introduction
1

Fill in the -**am** and -**ap** words.

WORD FAMILIES
-am, -ap

Hi!

-am	-ap
cl______	c______
h______	m______
sw______	n______

MAP

ZZZZZ

Color in each box when you complete an activity.

1 Introduction -am & -ap	2 Read & Write -am	3 Match & Find -am	4 Graph -am
5 Read & Write -ap	6 Match & Find -ap	7 Graph -ap	8 Review -am & -ap

Name: ____________________

Read the sentence.
Then write the words.

A boy named **Sam** saw a **clam** when he **swam**.

Sam Sam

clam clam

swam swam

Use the letters from the letter bank to make more **-am** words.

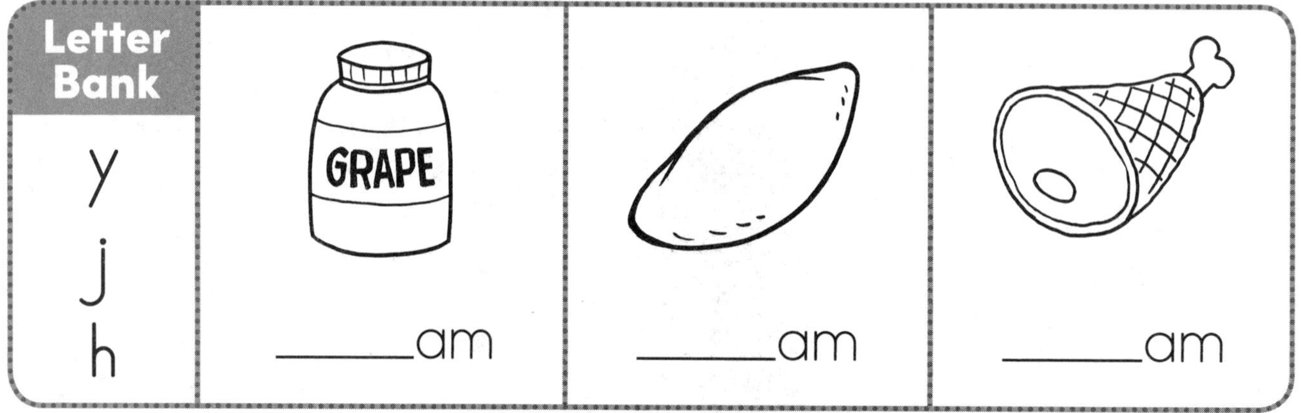

Name: ______________________________

Match the -**am** words to their pictures.

jam •

ham •

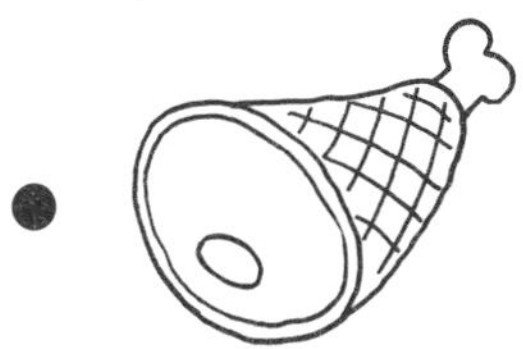

ram •

clam •

swam •

Find each -**am** word once.

Word Bank							
	y	c	h	a	m	t	a
ram	b	s	w	a	m	u	m
swam	c	l	a	m	f	p	e
ham	r	j	a	m	g	g	n
jam	u	g	c	b	r	a	m
clam							

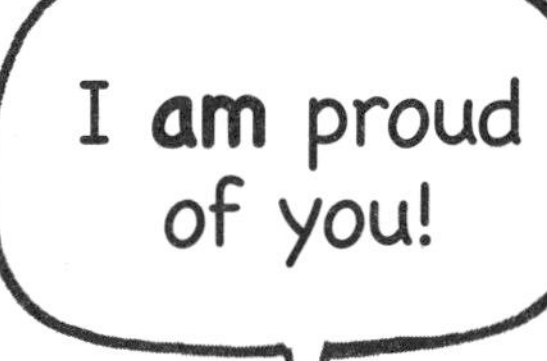

Name: ____

Count and graph the **-am** words.

clam jam jam ram

jam clam clam

ham jam ham

	ham	jam	ram	clam
4				
3				
2				
1				

I found this –am word the most times:

____

Name: ______________________________

Read the sentence.
Then write the words.

The **cap** with a **map** took a **nap**.

cap cap

map map

nap nap

Use the letters from the letter bank to make more **-ap** words.

Letter Bank			
c			
cl			
fl	____ap	____ap	____ap

WORD FAMILIES 6
Match & Find -ap
6

Name: ______________________________

Match the -**ap** words to their pictures.

cap •

lap •

map •

nap •

clap •

Find each -**ap** word once.

Word Bank							
clap	m	n	r	e	n	a	p
map	s	f	l	a	p	u	t
nap	k	m	a	p	g	z	e
lap	c	a	p	e	h	g	n
cap	u	g	c	l	a	p	o

WORD FAMILIES 6
Graph -ap
7

Name: ______________________________

Count and graph the -ap words.

Math is fun!

map clap
cap nap nap
map map cap
nap nap

	 cap	 map	 nap	 clap
4				
3				
2				
1				

I found this -ap word the most times:

____

Name: ______________________________

WORD FAMILIES 6
Review
-am & -ap
8

Use each -am and -ap word once to complete the story. Then read it aloud.

Word Bank	
-am	**-ap**
Sam	nap
clam	map
am	cap

Clam and Cap

Look at the __________.

It is on the __________!

They have a __________.

They see a dog __________

and a boy named __________.

"I __________ so happy!" said the cap.

"Me, too!" said the clam.

Name: ______________________________

Fill in the **-ill** and **-ip** words.

WORD FAMILIES
-ill, -ip

Color in each box when you complete an activity.

1 Introduction -ill & -ip	2 Read & Write -ill	3 Match & Find -ill	4 Graph -ill
5 Read & Write -ip	6 Match & Find -ip	7 Graph -ip	8 Review -ill & -ip

Name: ______________________________

Read the sentence.
Then write the words.

Jill **will** climb up the **hill**.

Jill Jill

will will

hill hill

Use the letters from the letter bank to make more **-ill** words.

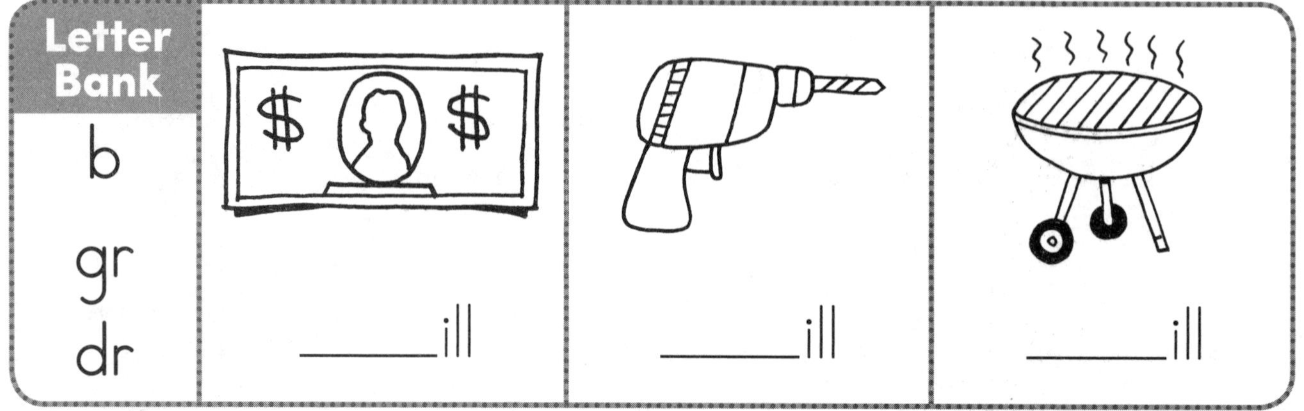

Name: ______________________________

Match the **-ill** words to their pictures.

hill •

bill •

grill •

drill •

quill •

• 

• 

• 

• 

• 

Find each **-ill** word once.

Word Bank							
drill	d	b	i	l	l	t	a
quill	b	e	d	r	i	l	l
bill	q	k	o	h	i	l	l
hill	r	a	q	u	i	l	l
grill	u	g	r	i	l	l	t

Name: ______________________________

Count and graph the -ill words.

Math is fun!

JILL

bill bill grill hill

grill hill bill

hill drill hill

	hill	bill	grill	drill
4				
3				
2				
1				

I found this –ill word the most times:

____

WORD FAMILIES 7
Read & Write -ip
5

Name: ______________________________

Read the sentence.
Then write the words.

Kip will take a **trip** on a **ship**.

Kip Kip

trip trip

ship ship

Use the letters from the letter bank to make more **-ip** words.

Letter Bank			
s l r	____ip	____ip	____ip

Name: ______________________________

Match the **-ip** words to their pictures.

lip •	• 
rip •	• 
ship •	• 
hip •	• 
dip •	• 

Find each **-ip** word once.

Word Bank							
lip	y	c	d	i	p	t	s
dip	b	s	h	i	p	u	x
ship	l	i	p	d	m	e	q
hip	n	a	s	z	r	i	p
rip	u	g	c	h	i	p	t

WORD FAMILIES 7
Graph -ip
7

Name: ______________________________

Count and graph the -ip words.

Math is fun!

rip lip lip rip slip slip rip lip rip ship

	 lip	 ship	 rip	 slip
4				
3				
2				
1				

I found this -ip word the most times:

____

WORD FAMILIES 7
Review -ill & -ip
8

Name: ____

Use each -ill and -ip word once to complete the story. Then read it aloud.

Word Bank	
-ill	**-ip**
will	Kip
thrill	ship
hill	trip

Jill and Kip

See the sailing ________.

________ is going to visit Jill.

Jill is on a ________!

"I ________ be there soon," says Kip.

Taking a ________

is such a ________!

Name: ______________________________

Fill in the -**ail** and -**ake** words.

-ail	-ake
sn______	sn______
p______	c______
m______	r______

Color in each box when you complete an activity.

1 Introduction -ail & -ake	2 Read & Write -ail	3 Match & Find -ail	4 Graph -ail
5 Read & Write -ake	6 Match & Find -ake	7 Graph -ake	8 Review -ail & -ake

Name: ______________________________

WORD FAMILIES 8
Read & Write -ail
2

Read the sentence.
Then write the words.

A **snail** named **Gail** lived in a **pail**.

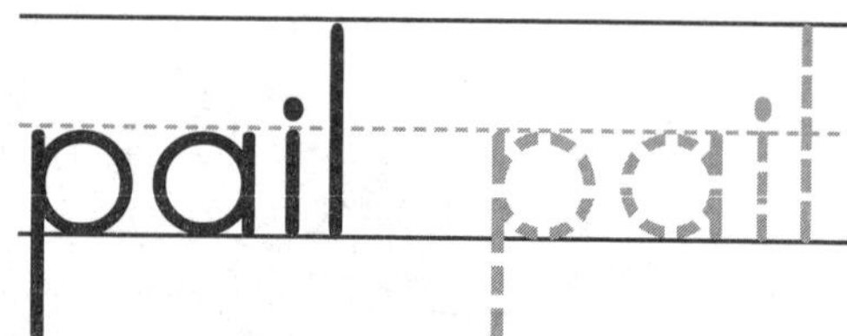

snail snail

Gail Gail

pail pail

Use the letters from the letter bank to make more -**ail** words.

Letter Bank			
n tr s	______ail	______ail	______ail

Name: ______________________________

Match the -**ail** words to their pictures.

snail •	• 
pail •	• 
tail •	• 
nail •	• 
rail •	• 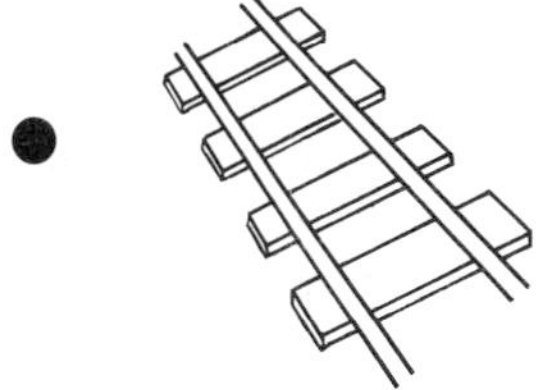

Find each -**ail** word once.

Word Bank							
pail	b	t	a	i	l	t	a
rail	n	a	i	l	z	u	g
tail	g	k	o	p	a	i	l
snail	s	r	a	i	l	g	n
nail	u	s	n	a	i	l	r

Name: ______________________________

Count and graph the **-ail** words.

	snail	quail	mail	sail
4				
3				
2				
1				

I found this –ail word the most times:

____

Name: ______________________________

Read the sentence.
Then write the words.

A **snake** named **Jake** jumped in a **lake**.

snake snake

Jake Jake

lake lake

Use the letters from the letter bank to make more **-ake** words.

Letter Bank			
r sh c	______ake	______ake	______ake

WORD FAMILIES 8
Match & Find
-ake
6

Name: ______________________________

Match the **-ake** words to their pictures.

snake •

cake •

lake •

flake •

rake •

Find each **-ake** word once.

Word Bank							
rake	y	c	a	k	e	t	b
flake	r	a	k	e	a	u	p
cake	s	n	a	k	e	p	r
snake	r	a	f	l	a	k	e
lake	u	l	a	k	e	s	t

Words **make** me happy!
JAKE

Name: ____

WORD FAMILIES 8
Graph -ake
7

Count and graph the **-ake** words.

Math is fun!

cake
shake
cake
lake
snake
shake
cake
cake
shake
lake

	snake	lake	shake	cake
4				
3				
2				
1				

I found this –ake word the most times:

____

Name: ______________________________

Use each **-ail** and **-ake** word once to complete the story. Then read it aloud.

Word Bank	
-ail	**-ake**
pail	Jake
trail	snake
snail	cake

Gail and Jake

Gail is a __________.

Jake is a __________.

Look! Jake baked a __________!

Then he slid along a __________.

When he got to Gail's __________,

__________ sang, "Happy Birthday to you!"

Name: ______________________________

Fill in the **-ee** and **-eep** words.

Color in each box when you complete an activity.

① Introduction -ee & -eep	② Read & Write -ee	③ Match & Find -ee	④ Graph -ee
⑤ Read & Write -eep	⑥ Match & Find -eep	⑦ Graph -eep	⑧ Review -ee & -eep

Name: ____________________

Read the sentence.
Then write the words.

Can you **see** the **bee** hiding in the **tree**?

see see

bee bee

tree tree

Use the letters from the letter bank to make more -ee words.

Letter Bank
gl
thr
kn
____ee
____ee
____ee

Name: ______________________________

Match the -ee words to their pictures.

bee •	•

tree •	•

knee •	• 

three •	• 

glee •	• 

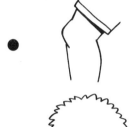

Find each -ee word once.

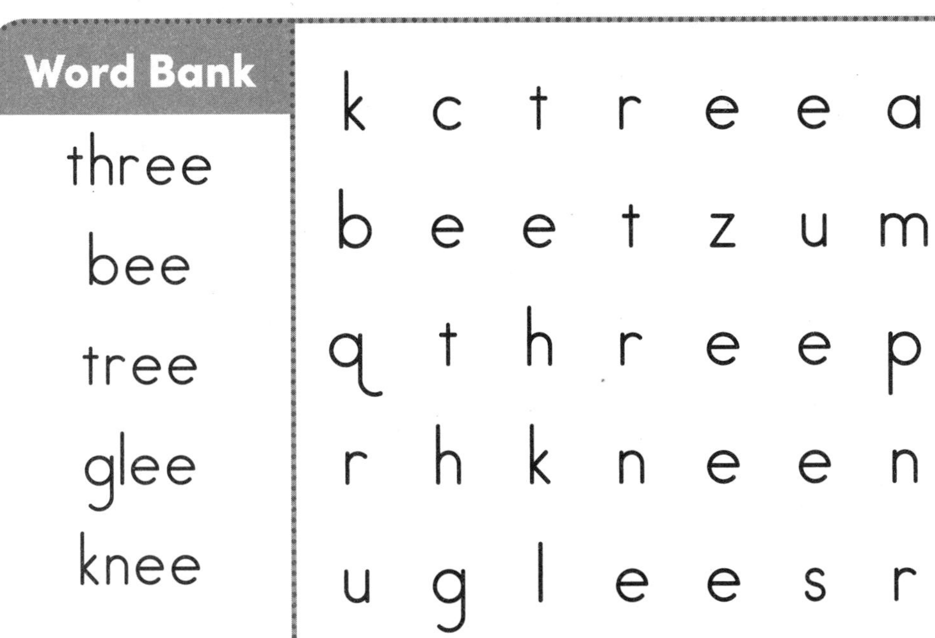

Word Bank							
three	k	c	t	r	e	e	a
bee	b	e	e	t	z	u	m
tree	q	t	h	r	e	e	p
glee	r	h	k	n	e	e	n
knee	u	g	l	e	e	s	r

Name: ______________________________

Count and graph the -ee words.

knee see bee bee knee see three see bee bee

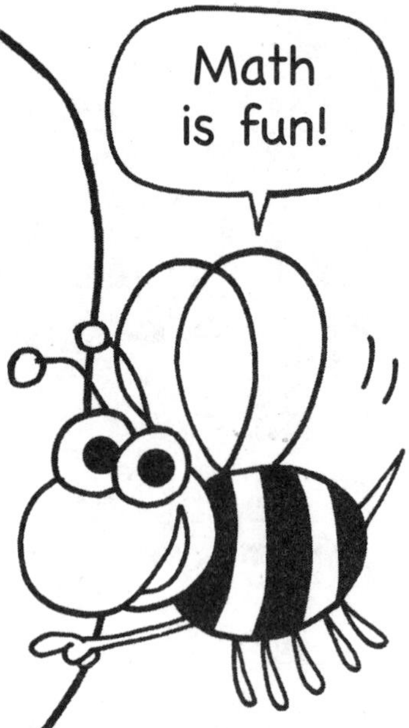

Math is fun!

	bee	see	knee	three
4				
3				
2				
1				

I found this –ee word the most times:

____

Name: ______________________________

Read the sentence.
Then write the words.

The **sheep** is in a **jeep**. Beep, **beep**!

sheep sheep

jeep jeep

beep beep

Use the letters from the letter bank to make more **-eep** words.

Letter Bank			
p sw sl	peep _____eep	_____eep	_____eep

WORD FAMILIES 9
Match & Find -eep
6

Name: ______________________________

Match the **-eep** words to their pictures.

sheep •   • 

jeep •   • 

sleep •   • 

sweep •   • 

peep •   • 

Find each **-eep** word once.

Word Bank							
jeep	y	c	p	e	e	p	a
sheep	s	g	s	w	e	e	p
peep	q	s	h	e	e	p	n
sleep	j	e	e	p	g	t	y
sweep	u	s	l	e	e	p	t

Name: ______________________________

Count and graph the **-eep** words.

	sheep	jeep	sweep	sleep
4				
3				
2				
1				

I found this –eep word the most times:

____

Name: ______________________________

WORD FAMILIES 9
Review
-ee & -eep
8

Use each -ee and -eep word once to complete the story. Then read it aloud.

Word Bank	
-ee	-eep
see	beep
bee	sheep
three	jeep

Bee and Sheep

See the striped ________!

See the white ________!

They are in a ________.

They ________ two birds

and ________ big bears.

Beep, ________!

Name: ______________________________

Fill in the -**ice** and -**ight** words.

Color in each box when you complete an activity.

1 Introduction -ice & -ight	2 Read & Write -ice	3 Match & Find -ice	4 Graph -ice
5 Read & Write -ight	6 Match & Find -ight	7 Graph -ight	8 Review -ice & -ight

Name: ______________________________

Read the sentence.
Then write the words.

The **nice** **mice** eat a bowl of **ice** cream.

nice nice

mice mice

ice ice

Use the letters from the letter bank to make more -ice words.

Letter Bank			
r d sl	______ice	______ice	______ice

WORD FAMILIES 10
Match & Find -ice
3

Name: ______________________________

Match the **-ice** words to their pictures.

mice •	•
ice •	•
rice •	• 
slice •	• 
dice •	• 

Find each **-ice** word once.

Word Bank							
slice	g	c	m	i	c	e	h
dice	b	e	d	i	c	e	m
rice	i	c	e	p	f	k	j
ice	r	a	s	l	i	c	e
mice	u	g	c	r	i	c	e

Name: ______________________________

Count and graph the -ice words.

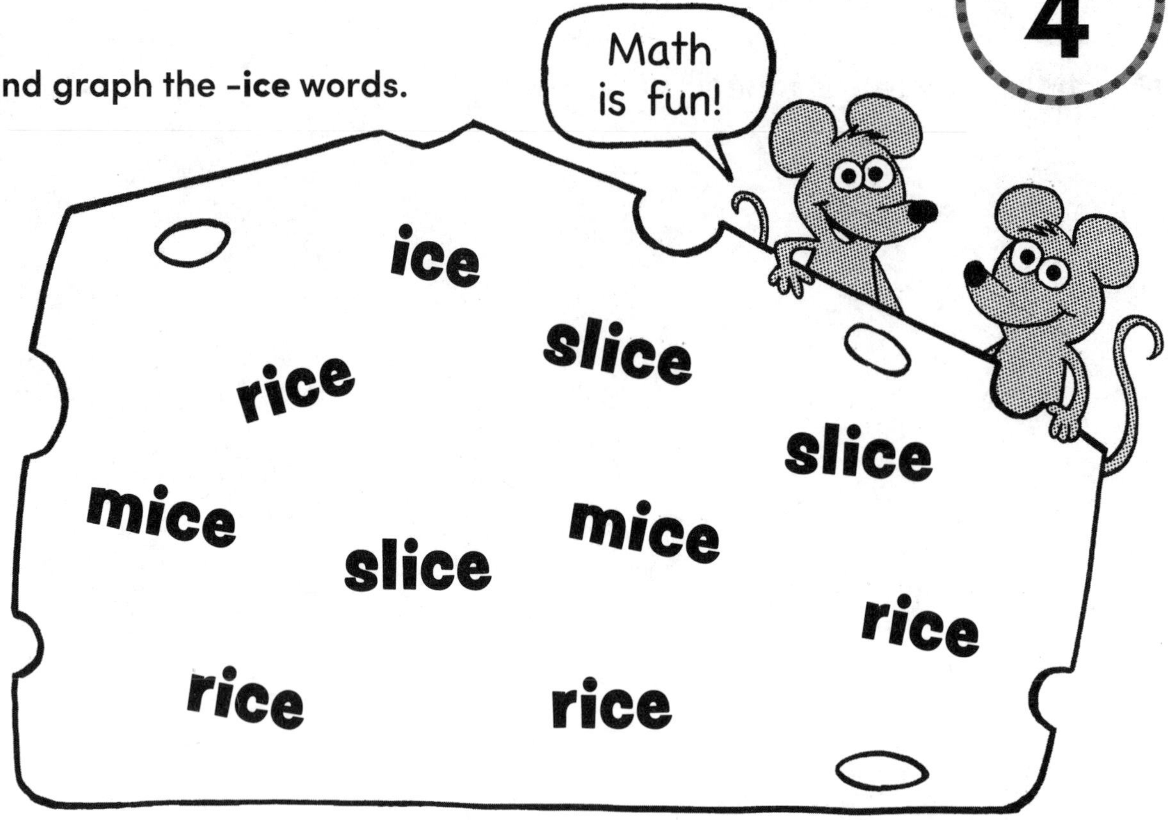

Math is fun!

ice

slice

rice

slice

mice

slice

mice

rice

rice

rice

	 mice	 rice	 slice	 ice
4				
3				
2				
1				

I found this -ice word the most times:

____

Name: ______________________________

Read the sentence.
Then write the words.

The **knight** saw a **bright** **light** in the sky.

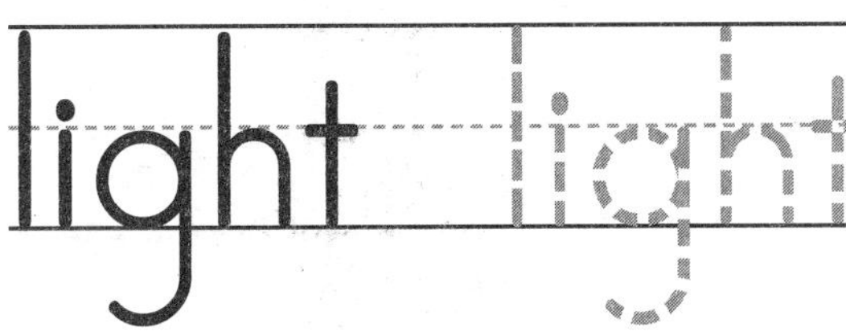

knight knight

bright bright

light light

Use the letters from the letter bank to make more -**ight** words.

Letter Bank			
n fl r	______ight	______ight	______ight

WORD FAMILIES 10
Match & Find -ight
6

Name: ____________________

Match the **-ight** words to their pictures.

knight •	• 
light •	• 
flight •	• 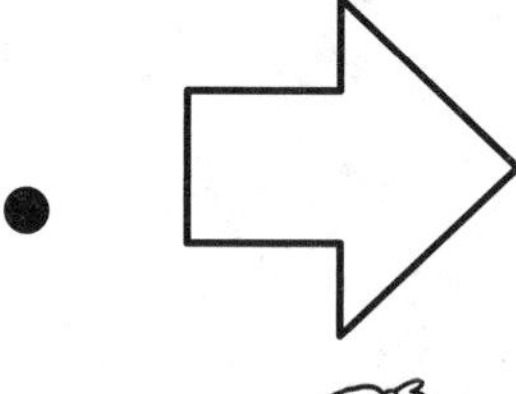
fight •	• 
right •	• 

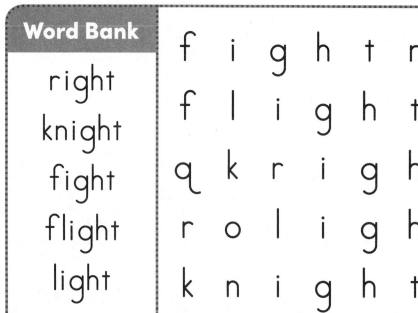

Find each **-ight** word once.

Word Bank

right
knight
fight
flight
light

f	i	g	h	t	r	a
f	l	i	g	h	t	d
q	k	r	i	g	h	t
r	o	l	i	g	h	t
k	n	i	g	h	t	z

Name: ____

Count and graph the **-ight** words.

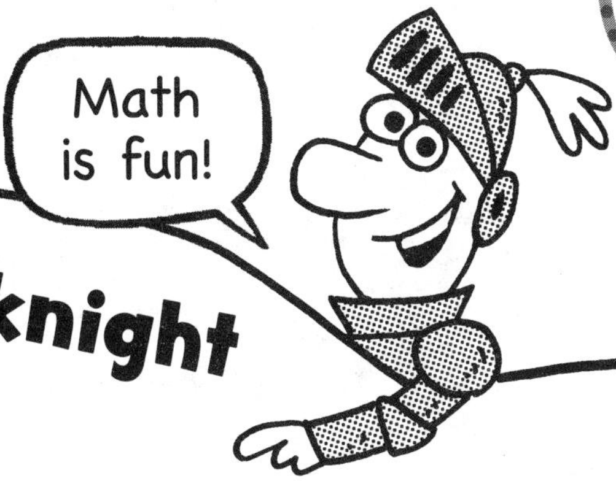

Math is fun!

right knight knight fight light light light knight fight knight

	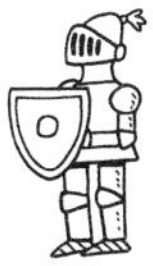 knight	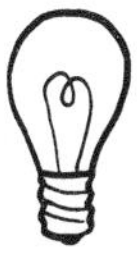 light	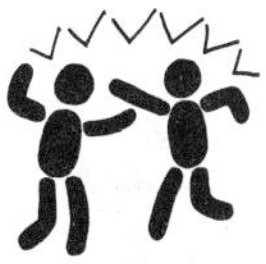 fight	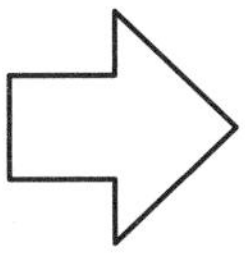 right
4				
3				
2				
1				

I found this –ight word the most times:

____

Name: ______________________________

WORD FAMILIES 10
Review
-ice & -ight
8

Use each **-ice** and **-ight** word once to complete the story. Then read it aloud.

Word Bank	
-ice	**-ight**
slice	right
mice	night
nice	knight

The Mice and Knight

The __________ are on the left.

The knight is on the __________.

It is a starry __________.

"Do you want a __________ of pizza?" ask the two mice.

"Thank you," says the __________.

"That would be so __________!"

Answer Key

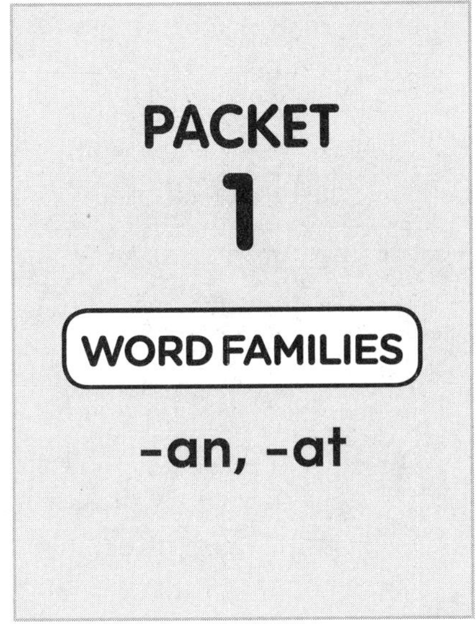

PACKET

1

WORD FAMILIES

-an, -at

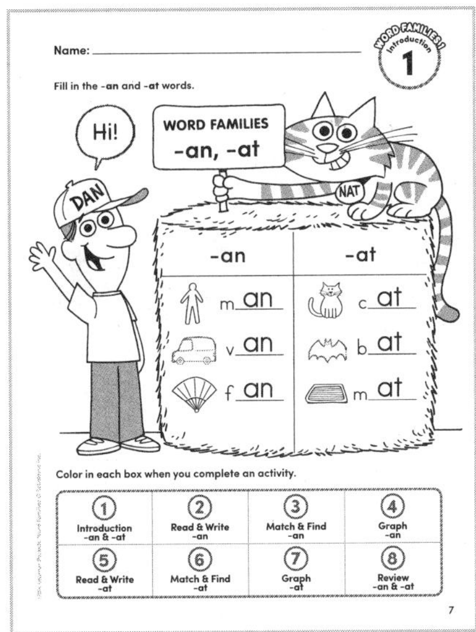

Name:

Introduction 1

Fill in the -an and -at words.

-an	-at
m an	c at
v an	b at
f an	m at

Color in each box when you complete an activity.

1 Introduction -an & -at	2 Read & Write -an	3 Match & Find -an	4 Graph -an
5 Read & Write -at	6 Match & Find -at	7 Graph -at	8 Review -an & -at

7

Name:

Read & Write -an 2

Read the sentence. Then write the words.

A man named Dan drives a big van.

man man man man

Dan Dan Dan Dan

van van van van van

Use the letters to make more -an words.

Letter Bank: p c f

p an | f an | c an

8

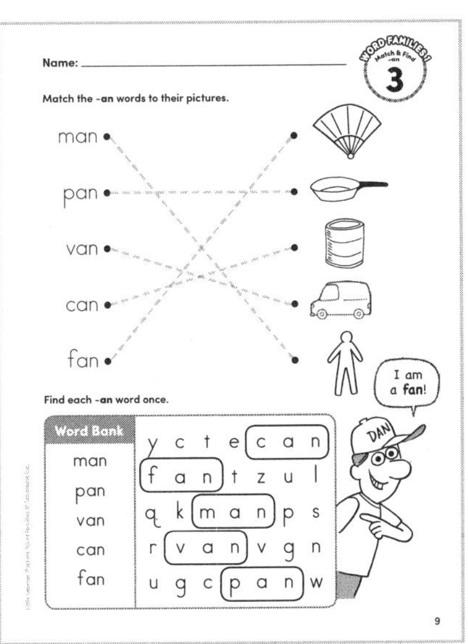

Name:

Match & Find -an 3

Match the -an words to their pictures.

man, pan, van, can, fan

Find each -an word once.

Word Bank						
man	y	c	t	e	c a n	
pan	f a n	t	z	u	l	
van	q	k	m a n	p	s	
can	r	v a n	v	g	n	
fan	u	g	c	p a n	w	

9

Name:

Graph -an 4

Count and graph the -an words.

	man	fan	tan	pan
4			■	
3			■	■
2		■	■	■
1	■	■	■	■

I found this -an word the most times: tan

10

Name:

Read & Write -at 5

Read the sentence. Then write the words.

The cat sat with a nice bat.

cat cat cat cat cat cat

sat sat sat sat sat sat

bat bat bat bat bat

Use the letters from the letter bank to make more -at words.

Letter Bank: p r h

r at | h at | p at

11

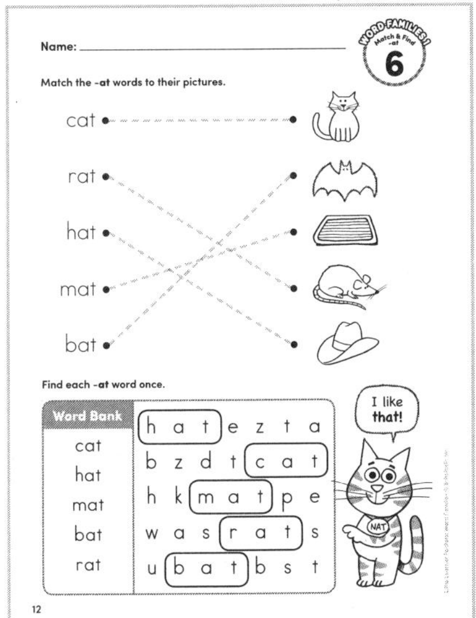

Name:

Match & Find -at 6

Match the -at words to their pictures.

cat, rat, hat, mat, bat

Find each -at word once.

Word Bank						
cat	h a t	e	z	t	a	
hat	b	z	d	t	c a t	
mat	h	k	m a t	p	e	
bat	w	a	s	r a t	s	
rat	u	b a t	b	s	t	

12

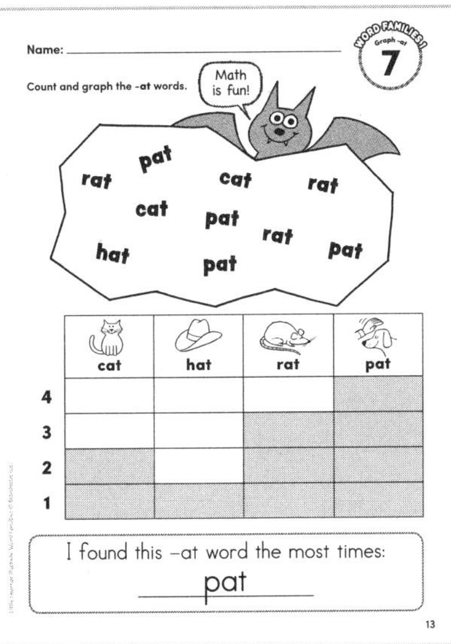

Name:

Graph -at 7

Count and graph the -at words.

	cat	hat	rat	pat
4				■
3			■	■
2	■		■	■
1	■	■	■	■

I found this -at word the most times: pat

13

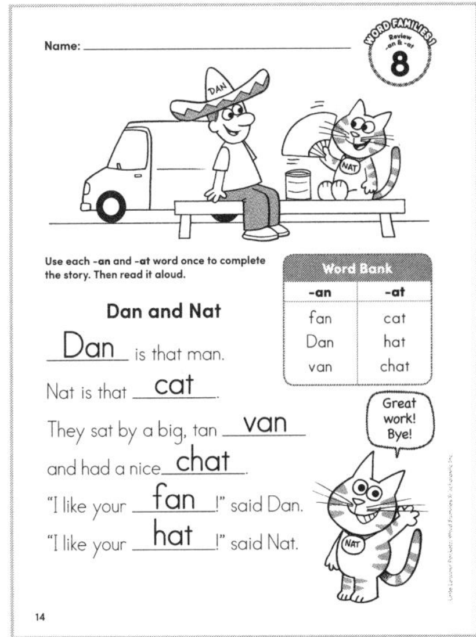

Name:

Review -an & -at 8

Use each -an and -at word once to complete the story. Then read it aloud.

Word Bank	
-an	-at
fan	cat
Dan	hat
van	chat

Dan and Nat

Dan is that man.

Nat is that cat.

They sat by a big, tan van

and had a nice chat.

"I like your fan!" said Dan.

"I like your hat!" said Nat.

14

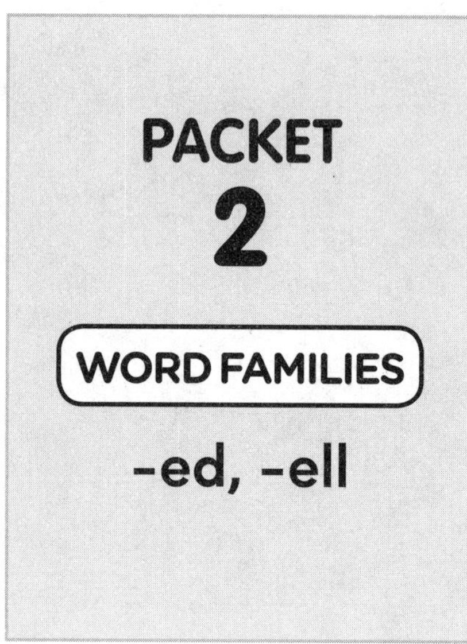
PACKET
2
WORD FAMILIES
-ed, -ell

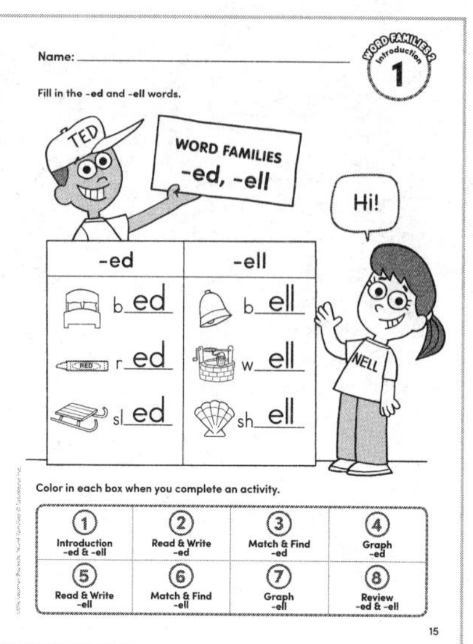
Name:
Fill in the -ed and -ell words.
WORD FAMILIES -ed, -ell
Hi!
-ed -ell
bed bell
red well
sled shell
Color in each box when you complete an activity.
1 Introduction -ed & -ell
2 Read & Write -ed
3 Match & Find -ed
4 Graph -ed
5 Read & Write -ell
6 Match & Find -ell
7 Graph -ell
8 Review -ed & -ell
15

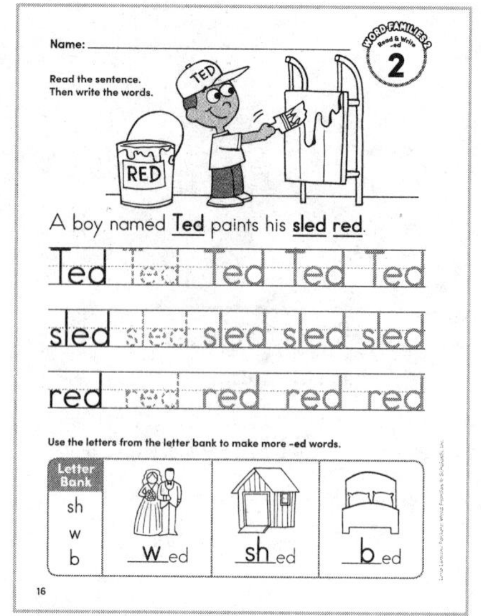
Name:
Read the sentence. Then write the words.
RED
A boy named Ted paints his sled red.
Ted Ted Ted Ted Ted
sled sled sled sled sled
red red red red red
Use the letters from the letter bank to make more -ed words.
Letter Bank
sh
w
b
wed shed bed
16

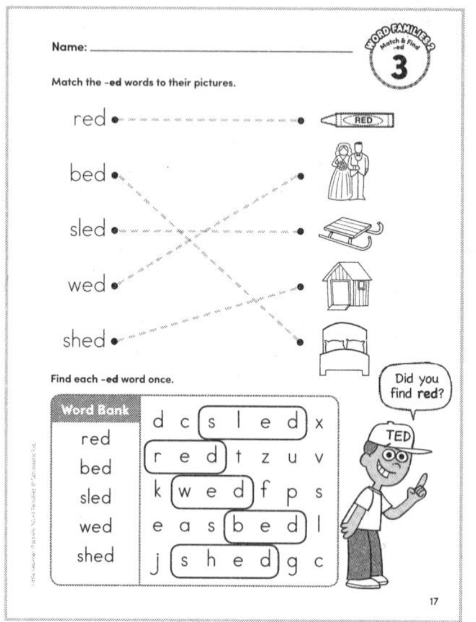
Name:
Match the -ed words to their pictures.
red
bed
sled
wed
shed
Find each -ed word once.
Did you find red?
Word Bank
red
bed
sled
wed
shed
17

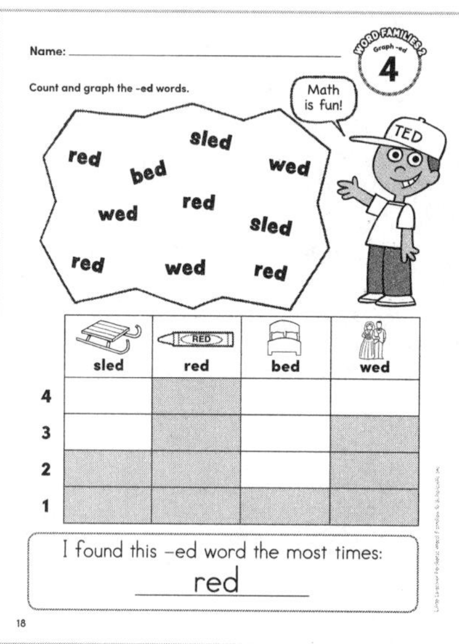
Name:
Count and graph the -ed words.
Math is fun!
red bed sled wed red wed sled red wed red
sled red bed wed
I found this -ed word the most times:
red
18

Name:
Read the sentence. Then write the words.
A girl named Nell has a shell and a bell.
Nell Nell Nell Nell Nell
shell shell shell shell
bell bell bell bell bell
Use the letters from the letter bank to make more -ell words.
Letter Bank
y
sm
w
yell smell well
19

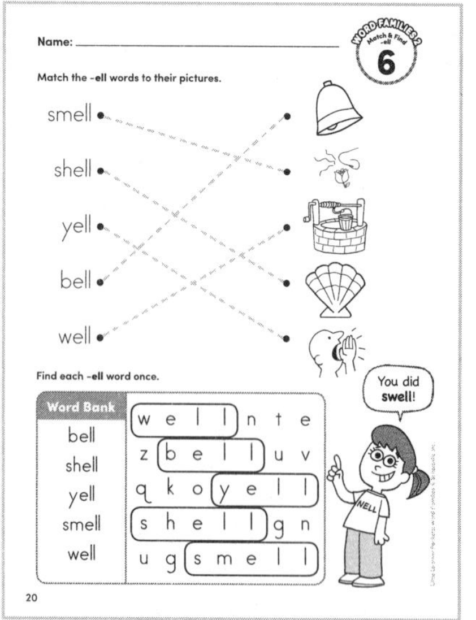
Name:
Match the -ell words to their pictures.
smell
shell
yell
bell
well
Find each -ell word once.
You did swell!
Word Bank
bell
shell
yell
smell
well
20

Name:
Count and graph the -ell words.
Math is fun!
sell shell sell smell shell shell bell bell sell shell
bell smell shell sell
I found this -ell word the most times:
shell
21

Name:
Use each -ed and -ell word once to complete the story. Then read it aloud.
Word Bank
-ed -ell
shed bell
Ted Nell
sled shell
Ted and Nell
His name is Ted.
He has a red sled.
Her name is Nell.
She has a sea shell
and a big bell.
Where will they keep their stuff?
Inside the shed!
Great work! Bye!
22

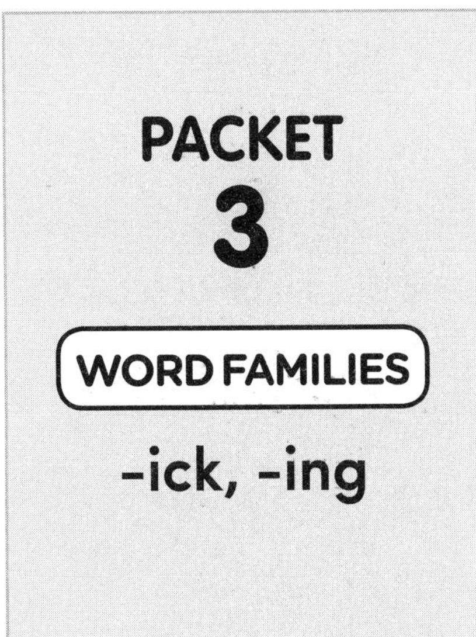
PACKET
3
WORD FAMILIES
-ick, -ing

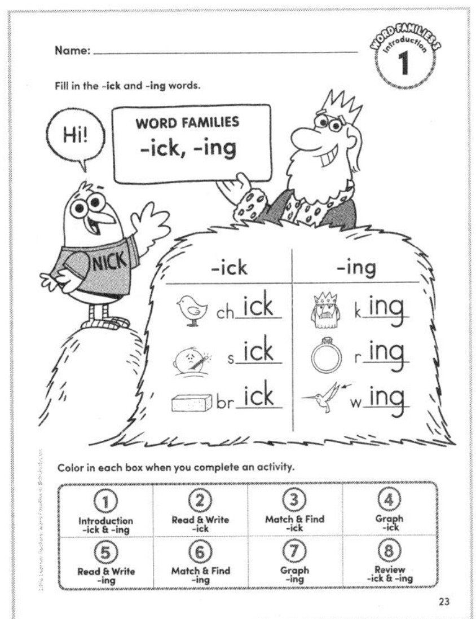
Name:
1
Fill in the -ick and -ing words.
Hi!
WORD FAMILIES
-ick, -ing
NICK
-ick
-ing
ch ick
k ing
s ick
r ing
br ick
w ing
Color in each box when you complete an activity.
1 Introduction -ick & -ing
2 Read & Write -ick
3 Match & Find -ick
4 Graph -ick
5 Read & Write -ing
6 Match & Find -ing
7 Graph -ing
8 Review -ick & -ing
23

Name:
2
Read the sentence.
Then write the words.
NICK
"I love to lick my lollipop!"
said a chick named Nick.
lick lick lick lick lick lick
chick chick chick chick
Nick Nick Nick Nick
Use the letters from the letter bank to make more -ick words.
Letter Bank
tr
k
st
k ick
tr ick
st ick
24

Name:
3
Match the -ick words to their pictures.
chick
stick
kick
brick
sick
Find each -ick word once.
You are slick!
Word Bank
sick
stick
chick
kick
brick
c a k i c k v
b z c h i c k
s i c k f p e
r s t i c k n
u g b r i c k
NICK
25

Name:
4
Count and graph the -ick words.
Math is fun!
kick
chick
kick
kick
brick
chick
trick
brick
kick
brick
NICK
chick
kick
brick
trick
4
3
2
1
I found this -ick word the most times:
kick
26

Name:
5
Read the sentence.
Then write the words.
The king loves to swing in the spring.
king king king king king
swing swing swing
spring spring spring
Use the letters from the letter bank to make more -ing words.
Letter Bank
r
str
w
r ing
str ing
w ing
27

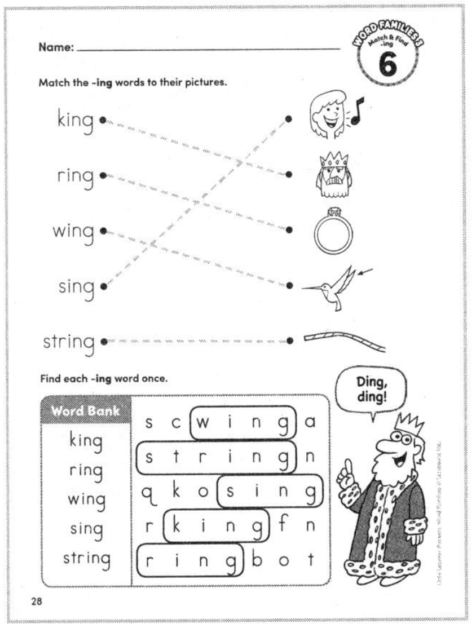
Name:
6
Match the -ing words to their pictures.
king
ring
wing
sing
string
Find each -ing word once.
Ding, ding!
Word Bank
king
ring
wing
sing
string
s c w i n g a
s t r i n g n
q k o s i n g
r k i n g f n
r i n g b o t
28

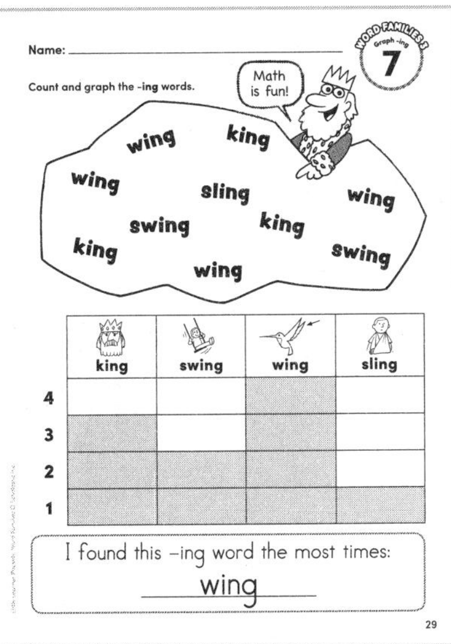
Name:
7
Count and graph the -ing words.
Math is fun!
wing
king
wing
sling
wing
swing
king
king
swing
wing
king
swing
wing
sling
4
3
2
1
I found this -ing word the most times:
wing
29

Name:
8
NICK
Use each -ick and -ing word once to complete the story. Then read it aloud.
Word Bank
-ick
-ing
pick
Nick
chick
swing
ring
spring
The Chick and the King
Zick, zing!
The season is spring!
The king wears a ring.
The chick has a lollipop.
His name is Nick.
"I will pick flowers,"
said the king.
"I will swing," said the chick.
Great work! Bye!
NICK
30

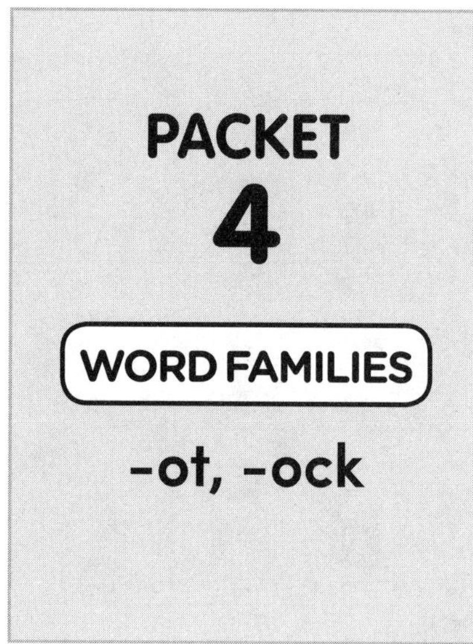
PACKET
4
WORD FAMILIES
-ot, -ock

Name:
Fill in the -ot and -ock words.
WORD FAMILIES
-ot, -ock
Hi!
-ot
-ock
d ot
p ot
t ot
cl ock
s ock
bl ock
Color in each box when you complete an activity.
1 Introduction -ot & -ock
2 Read & Write -ot
3 Match & Find -ot
4 Graph -ot
5 Read & Write -ock
6 Match & Find -ock
7 Graph -ock
8 Review -ot & -ock
31

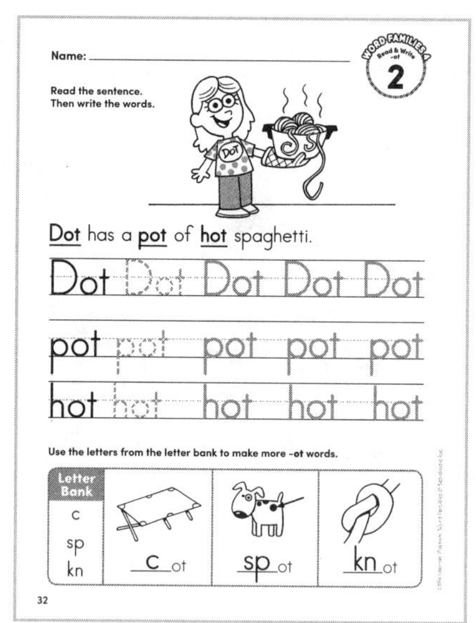
Name:
Read the sentence.
Then write the words.
Dot has a pot of hot spaghetti.
Dot Dot Dot Dot Dot
pot pot pot pot pot
hot hot hot hot hot
Use the letters from the letter bank to make more -ot words.
Letter Bank
c
sp
kn
c ot
sp ot
kn ot
32

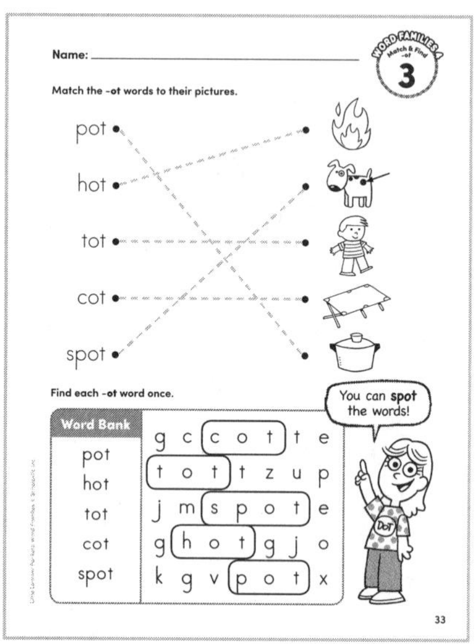
Name:
Match the -ot words to their pictures.
pot
hot
tot
cot
spot
Find each -ot word once.
You can spot the words!
Word Bank
pot
hot
tot
cot
spot
g c c o t t e
t o t t z u p
j m s p o t e
g h o t g j o
k g v p o t x
33

Name:
Count and graph the -ot words.
Math is fun!
spot
spot
knot
pot
knot
tot
tot
knot
spot
knot
pot
spot
tot
knot
4
3
2
1
I found this -ot word the most times:
knot
34

Name:
Read the sentence.
Then write the words.
TICK, TOCK!
The clock on the rock says, "Tick, tock."
clock clock clock clock
rock rock rock rock
tock tock tock tock
Use the letters from the letter bank to make more -ock words.
Letter Bank
s
kn
bl
kn ock
bl ock
s ock
35

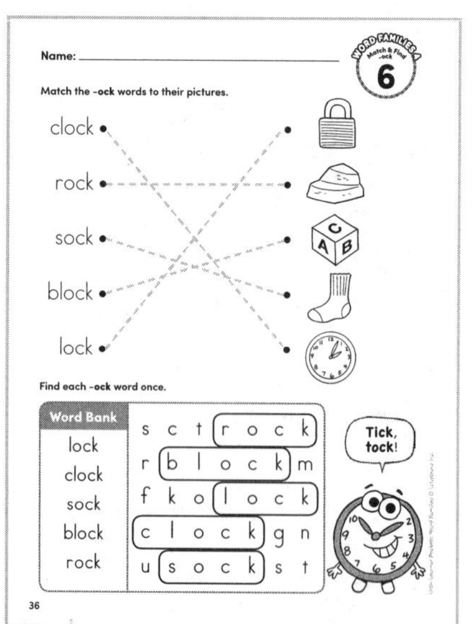
Name:
Match the -ock words to their pictures.
clock
rock
sock
block
lock
Find each -ock word once.
Tick, tock!
Word Bank
lock
clock
sock
block
rock
s c t r o c k
r b l o c k m
f k o l o c k
c l o c k g n
u s o c k s t
36

Name:
Count and graph the -ock words.
Math is fun!
dock
rock
dock
rock
lock
clock
rock
lock
dock
rock
clock
lock
rock
dock
4
3
2
1
I found this -ock word the most times:
rock
37

Name:
RING! RING!
Use each -ot and -ock word once to complete the story. Then read it aloud.
Word Bank
-ot
-ock
not
Dot
got
rock
clock
tock
Dot and the Clock
Dot has a problem.
She does not like to wake up.
So she got a new clock.
At night, the clock says, "Tick, tock."
But in the morning, it says, "RING, RING!"
Hooray! The clock wakes her up.
"Clock, you rock!" says Dot.
38

PACKET
5
WORD FAMILIES
-ug, -uck

Name:
Fill in the -ug and -uck words.
Hi!
WORD FAMILIES
-ug, -uck
TUG
CHUCK
-ug
-uck
bug
duck
jug
buck
mug
cluck
Color in each box when you complete an activity.
1 Introduction -ug & -uck
2 Read & Write -ug
3 Match & Find -ug
4 Graph -ug
5 Read & Write -uck
6 Match & Find -uck
7 Graph -uck
8 Review -ug & -uck
39

Name:
2
Read the sentence.
Then write the words.
TUG'S MUG
A bug named Tug is in a mug.
bug bug bug bug bug
Tug Tug Tug Tug Tug
mug mug mug mug
Use the letters from the letter bank to make more -ug words.
Letter Bank
j
pl
r
jug
rug
plug
40

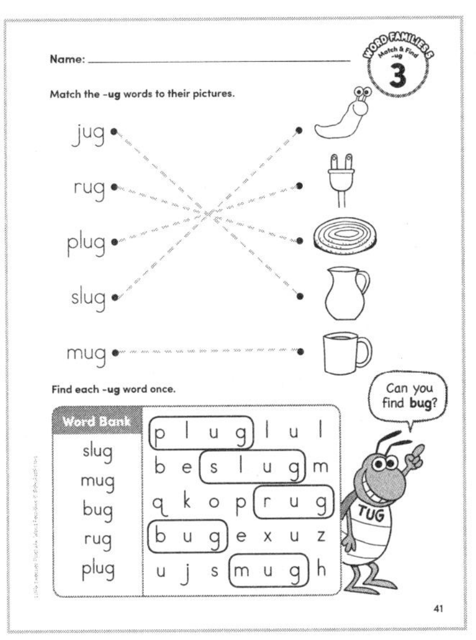
Name:
3
Match the -ug words to their pictures.
jug
rug
plug
slug
mug
Find each -ug word once.
Can you find bug?
Word Bank
slug
mug
bug
rug
plug
p l u g l u l
b e s l u g m
q k o p r u g
b u g e x u z
u j s m u g h
TUG
41

Name:
4
Count and graph the -ug words.
Math is fun!
rug
mug
pug
pug
bug
bug
mug
mug
pug
pug
TUG
bug
mug
rug
pug
4
3
2
1
I found this -ug word the most times:
pug
42

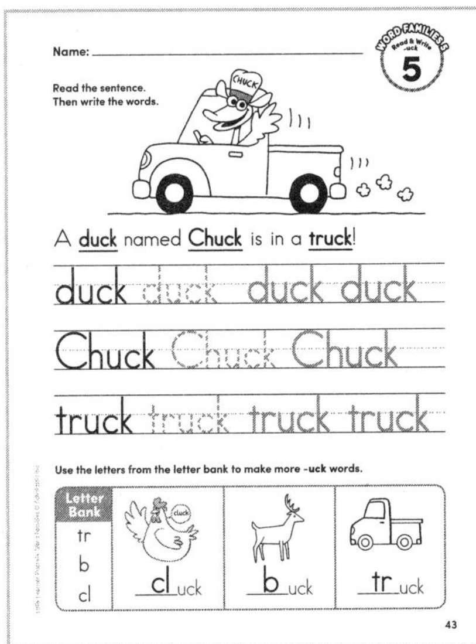
Name:
5
Read the sentence.
Then write the words.
CHUCK
A duck named Chuck is in a truck!
duck duck duck duck
Chuck Chuck Chuck
truck truck truck truck
Use the letters from the letter bank to make more -uck words.
Letter Bank
tr
b
cl
cluck
buck
truck
43

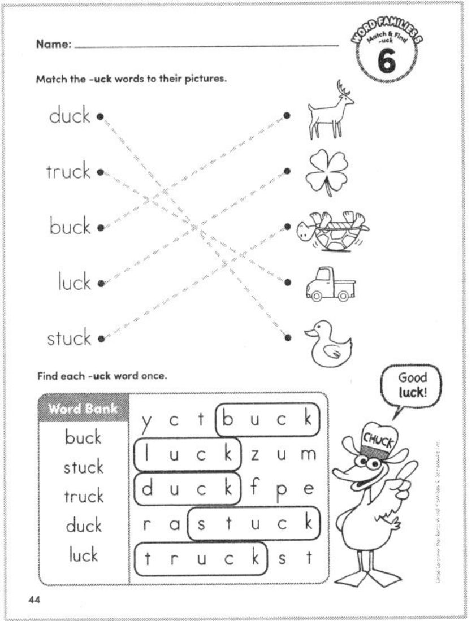
Name:
6
Match the -uck words to their pictures.
duck
truck
buck
luck
stuck
Find each -uck word once.
Good luck!
Word Bank
buck
stuck
truck
duck
luck
y c t b u c k
l u c k z u m
d u c k f p e
r a s t u c k
t r u c k s t
CHUCK
44

Name:
7
Count and graph the -uck words.
Math is fun!
truck
luck
cluck
truck
duck
duck
duck
duck
truck
luck
duck
luck
truck
cluck
4
3
2
1
I found this -uck word the most times:
duck
45

Name:
8
CHUCK
TUG'S MUG
Use each -ug and -uck word once to complete the story. Then read it aloud.
Word Bank
-ug
-uck
mug
jug
bug
duck
Chuck
truck
Tug and Chuck
Tug is a bug.
Chuck is a duck.
Chuck drove his truck
over to see Tug.
Did Chuck find Tug
in the mug? No!
Tug was in the jug!
Great work! Bye!
TUG
46

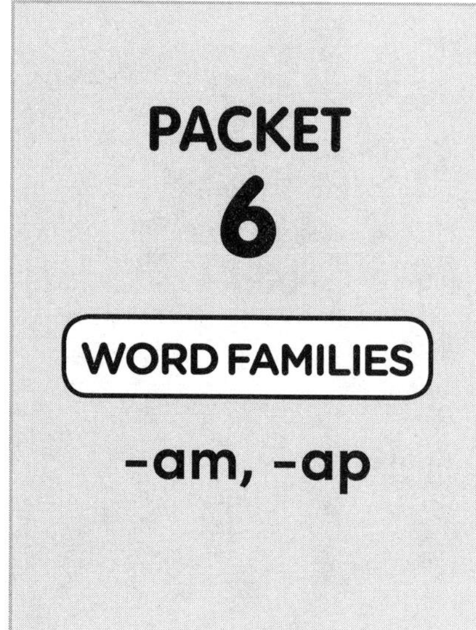
PACKET 6
WORD FAMILIES
-am, -ap

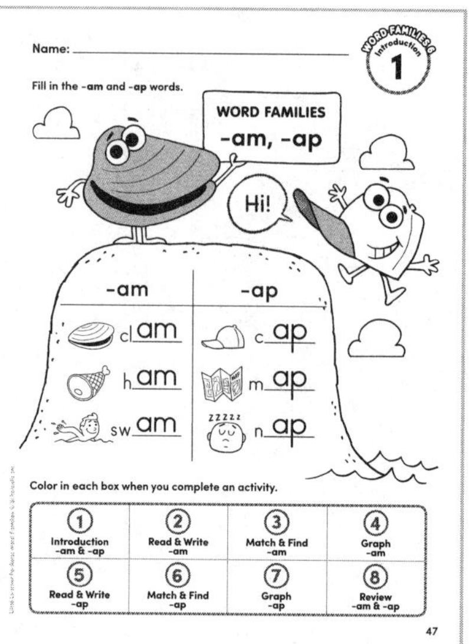
Name: ______

WORD FAMILIES Introduction 1

Fill in the -am and -ap words.

-am	-ap
clam	cap
ham	map
swam	nap

Color in each box when you complete an activity.

1 Introduction -am & -ap	2 Read & Write -am	3 Match & Find -am	4 Graph -am
5 Read & Write -ap	6 Match & Find -ap	7 Graph -ap	8 Review -am & -ap

47

Name: ______

WORD FAMILIES Read & Write -am 2

Read the sentence. Then write the words.

A boy named Sam saw a clam when he swam.

Sam Sam Sam Sam

clam clam clam clam

swam swam swam

Use the letters from the letter bank to make more -am words.

Letter Bank: y, j, h

jam · yam · ham

48

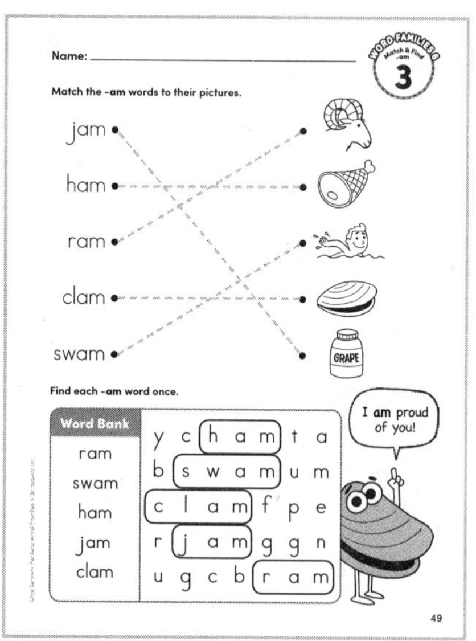
Name: ______

WORD FAMILIES Match & Find -am 3

Match the -am words to their pictures.

jam, ham, ram, clam, swam

Find each -am word once.

Word Bank: ram, swam, ham, jam, clam

y c h a m t a
b s w a m u m
c l a m f p e
r j a m g g n
u g c b r a m

49

Name: ______

WORD FAMILIES Graph -am 4

Count and graph the -am words.

clam jam jam ram
jam clam clam
ham jam ham

	ham	jam	ram	clam
4				
3				
2				
1				

I found this -am word the most times: jam

50

Name: ______

WORD FAMILIES Read & Write -ap 5

Read the sentence. Then write the words.

The cap with a map took a nap.

cap cap cap cap cap

map map map map

nap nap nap nap nap

Use the letters from the letter bank to make more -ap words.

Letter Bank: c, cl, fl

clap · flap · cap

51

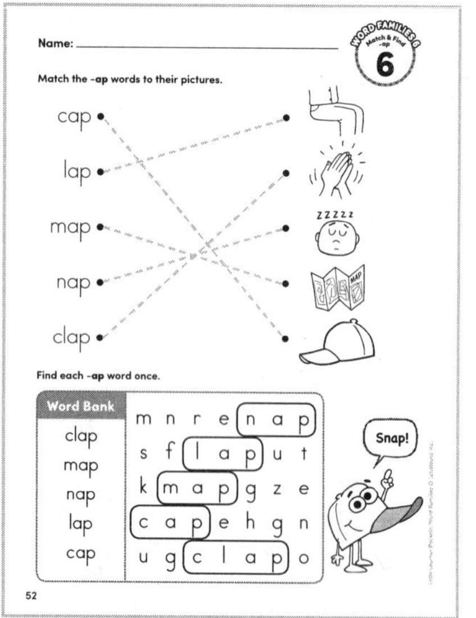
Name: ______

WORD FAMILIES Match & Find -ap 6

Match the -ap words to their pictures.

cap, lap, map, nap, clap

Find each -ap word once.

Word Bank: clap, map, nap, lap, cap

m n r e n a p
s f l a p u t
k m a p g z e
c a p e h g n
u g c l a p o

52

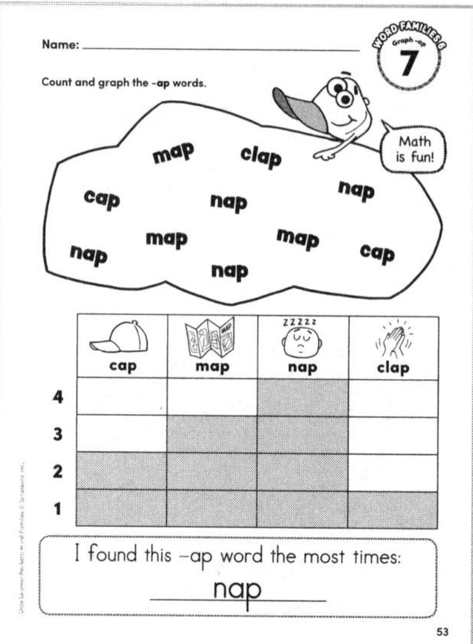
Name: ______

WORD FAMILIES Graph -ap 7

Count and graph the -ap words.

map clap
cap nap nap
map map cap
nap nap

	cap	map	nap	clap
4				
3				
2				
1				

I found this -ap word the most times: nap

53

Name: ______

WORD FAMILIES Review -am & -ap 8

Use each -am and -ap word once to complete the story. Then read it aloud.

Word Bank	
-am	-ap
Sam	nap
clam	map
am	cap

Clam and Cap

Look at the cap.
It is on the clam!
They have a map.
They see a dog nap
and a boy named Sam.
"I am so happy!" said the cap.
"Me, too!" said the clam.

54

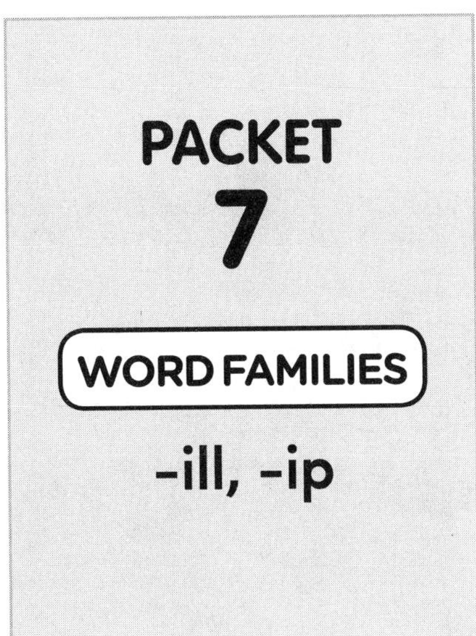

PACKET
7
WORD FAMILIES
-ill, -ip

Name:
Fill in the -ill and -ip words.
WORD FAMILIES
-ill, -ip
-ill
-ip
h ill
gr ill
sp ill
d ip
l ip
ch ip
Hi!
Hi!
JILL
KIP
Color in each box when you complete an activity.
1 Introduction -ill & -ip
2 Read & Write -ill
3 Match & Find -ill
4 Graph -ill
5 Read & Write -ip
6 Match & Find -ip
7 Graph -ip
8 Review -ill & -ip
55

Name:
2
Read the sentence.
Then write the words.
Jill will climb up the hill.
Jill Jill Jill Jill Jill Jill
will will will will will will
hill hill hill hill hill hill
Use the letters from the letter bank to make more -ill words.
Letter Bank
b
gr
dr
b ill
dr ill
gr ill
56

Name:
3
Match the -ill words to their pictures.
hill
bill
grill
drill
quill
Find each -ill word once.
You will find all the words!
Word Bank
drill
quill
bill
hill
grill
d b i l l t a
b e d r i l l
q k o h i l l
r a q u i l l
u g r i l l t
57

Name:
4
Count and graph the -ill words.
Math is fun!
bill
bill
grill
hill
grill
hill
bill
hill
drill
hill
hill
bill
grill
drill
4
3
2
1
I found this -ill word the most times:
hill
58

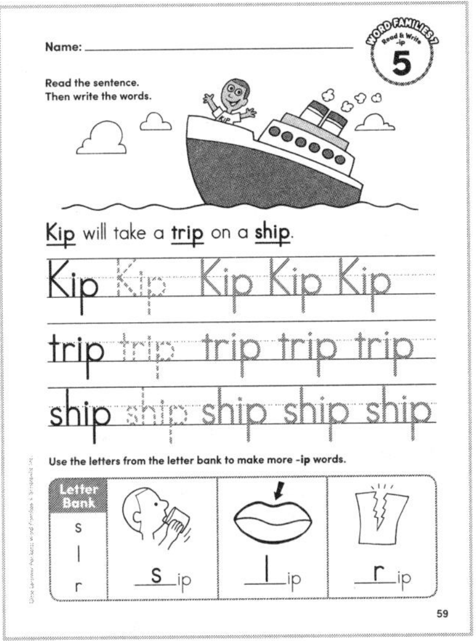

Name:
5
Read the sentence.
Then write the words.
Kip will take a trip on a ship.
Kip Kip Kip Kip Kip
trip trip trip trip trip
ship ship ship ship ship
Use the letters from the letter bank to make more -ip words.
Letter Bank
s
l
r
s ip
l ip
r ip
59

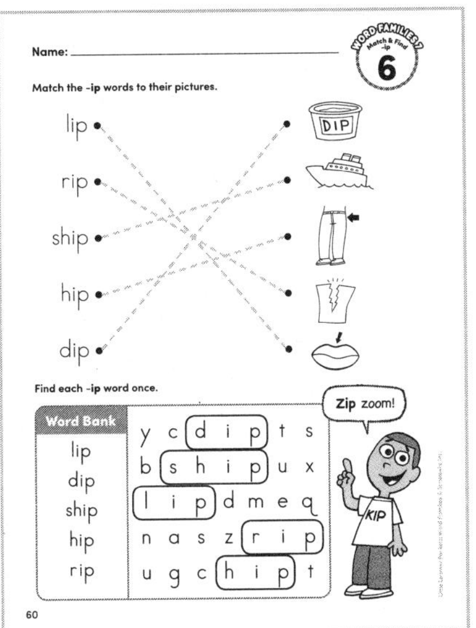

Name:
6
Match the -ip words to their pictures.
lip
rip
ship
hip
dip
DIP
Find each -ip word once.
Zip zoom!
Word Bank
lip
dip
ship
hip
rip
y c d i p t s
b s h i p u x
l i p d m e q
n a s z r i p
u g c h i p t
60

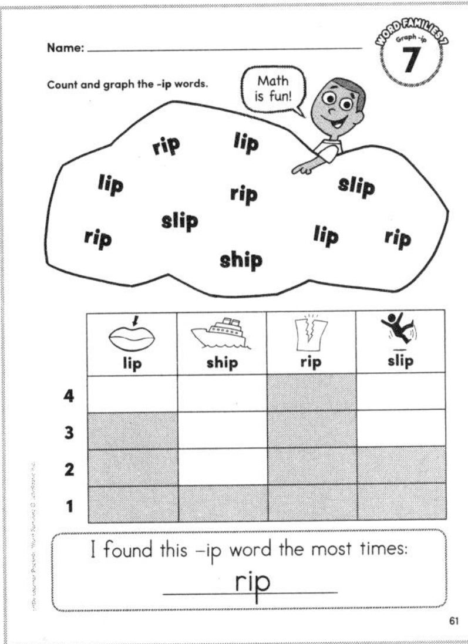

Name:
7
Count and graph the -ip words.
Math is fun!
rip
lip
lip
rip
slip
slip
rip
lip
rip
ship
lip
ship
rip
slip
4
3
2
1
I found this -ip word the most times:
rip
61

Name:
8
I will be there soon!
Use each -ill and -ip word once to complete the story. Then read it aloud.
Word Bank
-ill
-ip
will
thrill
hill
Kip
ship
trip
Jill and Kip
See the sailing ship.
Kip is going to visit Jill.
Jill is on a hill!
"I will be there soon," says Kip.
Taking a trip
is such a thrill!
Great work! Bye!
62

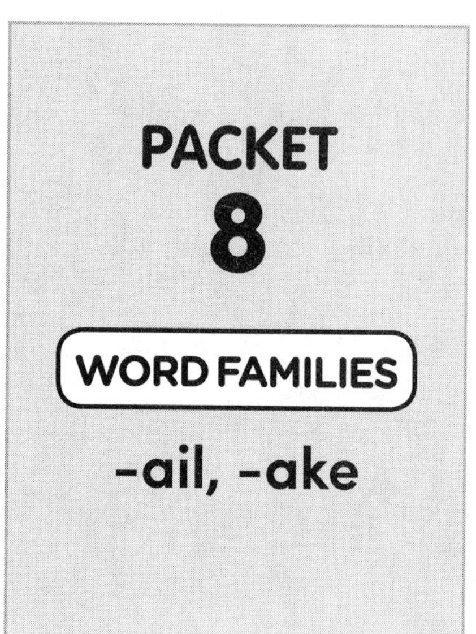
PACKET
8
WORD FAMILIES
-ail, -ake

Name:
WORD FAMILIES 8 Introduction
1
Fill in the -ail and -ake words.
GAIL
WORD FAMILIES
-ail, -ake
Hi!
JAKE
-ail
-ake
sn ail
p ail
m ail
sn ake
c ake
r ake
Color in each box when you complete an activity.
1 Introduction -ail & -ake
2 Read & Write -ail
3 Match & Find -ail
4 Graph -ail
5 Read & Write -ake
6 Match & Find -ake
7 Graph -ake
8 Review -ail & -ake
63

Name:
WORD FAMILIES 8 Read & Write -ail
2
Read the sentence.
Then write the words.
GAIL
A snail named Gail lived in a pail.
snail snail snail snail
Gail Gail Gail Gail
pail pail pail pail pail
Use the letters from the letter bank to make more -ail words.
Letter Bank
n
tr
s
s ail
n ail
tr ail
64

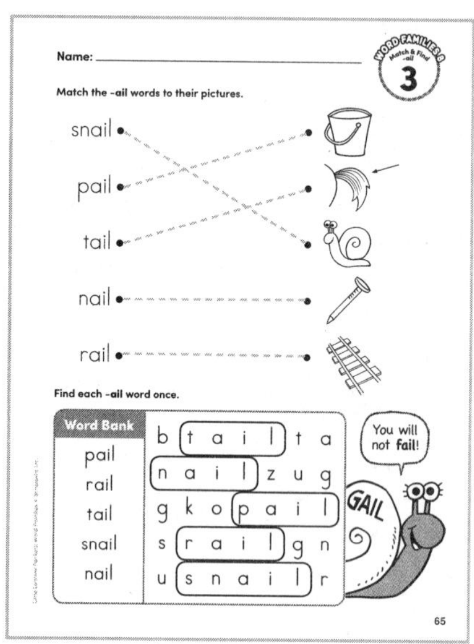
Name:
WORD FAMILIES 8 Match & Find -ail
3
Match the -ail words to their pictures.
snail
pail
tail
nail
rail
Find each -ail word once.
Word Bank
pail
rail
tail
snail
nail
b t a i l t a
n a i l z u g
g k o p a i l
s r a i l g n
u s n a i l r
You will not fail!
GAIL
65

Name:
WORD FAMILIES 8 Graph -ail
4
Count and graph the -ail words.
mail
sail
sail
snail
snail
sail
quail
mail
snail
sail
Math is fun!
GAIL
snail
quail
mail
sail
4
3
2
1
I found this -ail word the most times:
sail
66

Name:
WORD FAMILIES 8 Read & Write -ake
5
Read the sentence.
Then write the words.
JAKE
A snake named Jake jumped in a lake.
snake snake snake
Jake Jake Jake Jake
lake lake lake lake
Use the letters from the letter bank to make more -ake words.
Letter Bank
r
sh
c
r ake
c ake
sh ake
67

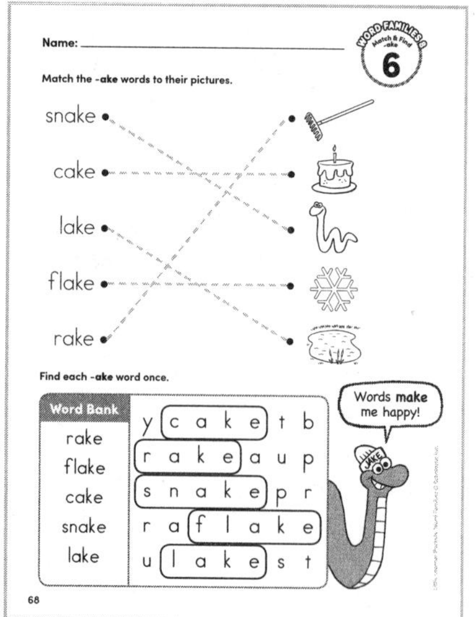
Name:
WORD FAMILIES 8 Match & Find -ake
6
Match the -ake words to their pictures.
snake
cake
lake
flake
rake
Find each -ake word once.
Word Bank
rake
flake
cake
snake
lake
y c a k e t b
r a k e a u p
s n a k e p r
r a f l a k e
u l a k e s t
Words make me happy!
JAKE
68

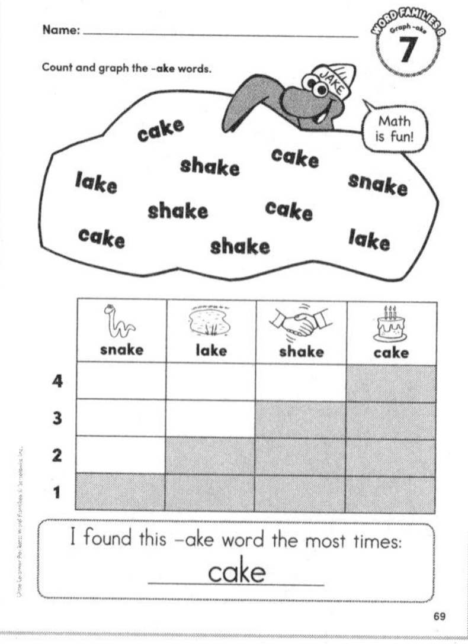
Name:
WORD FAMILIES 8 Graph -ake
7
Count and graph the -ake words.
JAKE
Math is fun!
cake
shake
cake
lake
snake
shake
cake
cake
shake
lake
snake
lake
shake
cake
4
3
2
1
I found this -ake word the most times:
cake
69

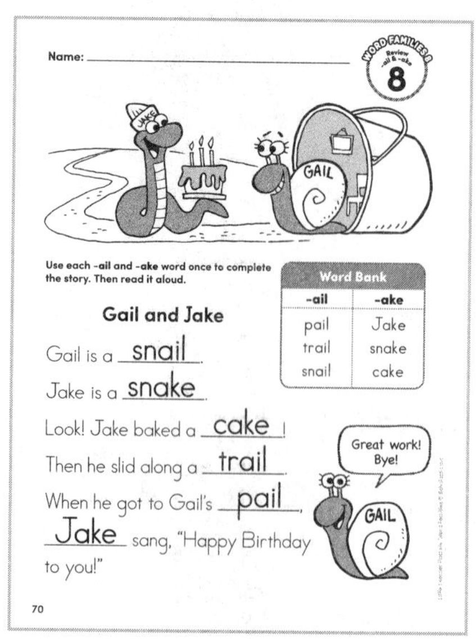
Name:
WORD FAMILIES 8 Review -ail & -ake
8
JAKE
GAIL
Use each -ail and -ake word once to complete the story. Then read it aloud.
Word Bank
-ail
-ake
pail
trail
snail
Jake
snake
cake
Gail and Jake
Gail is a snail.
Jake is a snake.
Look! Jake baked a cake!
Then he slid along a trail.
When he got to Gail's pail,
Jake sang, "Happy Birthday to you!"
Great work! Bye!
GAIL
70

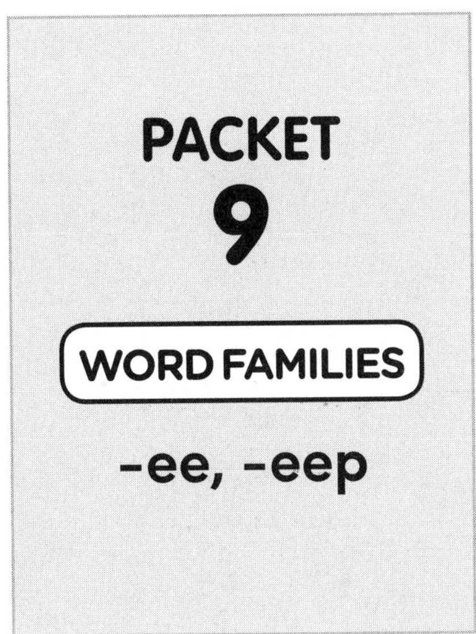
PACKET 9
WORD FAMILIES
-ee, -eep

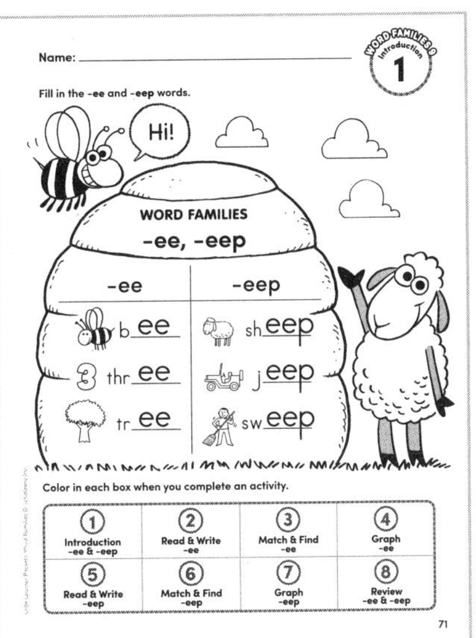
Name:
Word Families Introduction 1
Fill in the -ee and -eep words.
Hi!
WORD FAMILIES
-ee, -eep

-ee	-eep
b ee	sh eep
thr ee	j eep
tr ee	sw eep

Color in each box when you complete an activity.

1 Introduction -ee & -eep	2 Read & Write -ee	3 Match & Find -ee	4 Graph -ee
5 Read & Write -eep	6 Match & Find -eep	7 Graph -eep	8 Review -ee & -eep

71

Name:
Word Families Read & Write -ee 2
Read the sentence. Then write the words.
Can you see the bee hiding in the tree?
see see see see see
bee bee bee bee bee
tree tree tree tree
Use the letters from the letter bank to make more -ee words.
Letter Bank: gl, thr, kn
kn ee | gl ee | thr ee
72

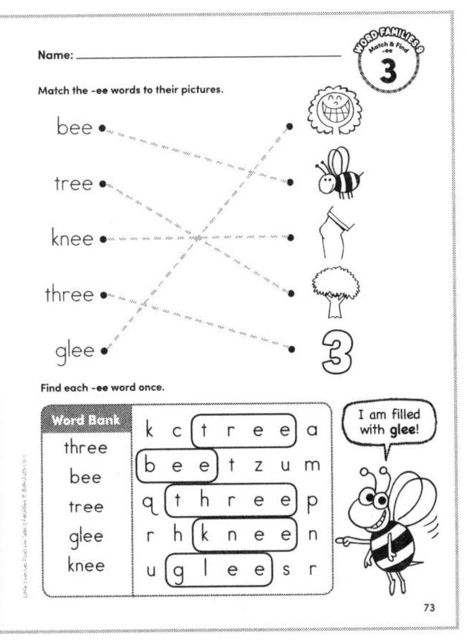
Name:
Word Families Match & Find -ee 3
Match the -ee words to their pictures.
bee
tree
knee
three
glee
Find each -ee word once.
Word Bank: three, bee, tree, glee, knee

k	c	t	r	e	e	a
b	e	e	t	z	u	m
q	t	h	r	e	e	p
r	h	k	n	e	e	n
u	g	l	e	e	s	r

I am filled with glee!
73

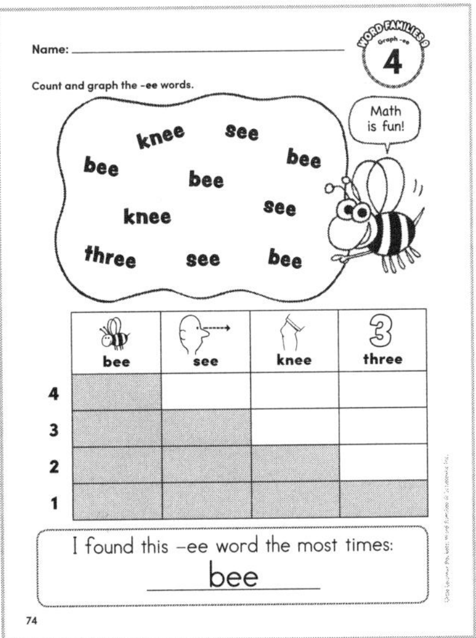
Name:
Word Families Graph -ee 4
Count and graph the -ee words.
knee see bee bee see knee bee three see bee
Math is fun!

	bee	see	knee	three
4				
3				
2				
1				

I found this -ee word the most times: bee
74

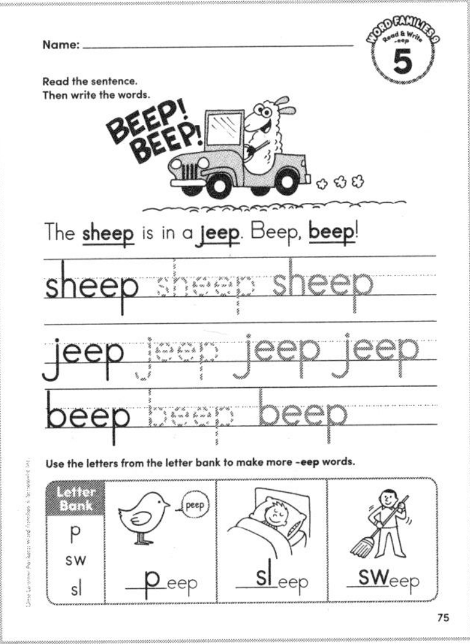
Name:
Word Families Read & Write -eep 5
Read the sentence. Then write the words.
BEEP! BEEP!
The sheep is in a jeep. Beep, beep!
sheep sheep sheep
jeep jeep jeep jeep
beep beep beep
Use the letters from the letter bank to make more -eep words.
Letter Bank: p, sw, sl
peep
p eep | sl eep | sw eep
75

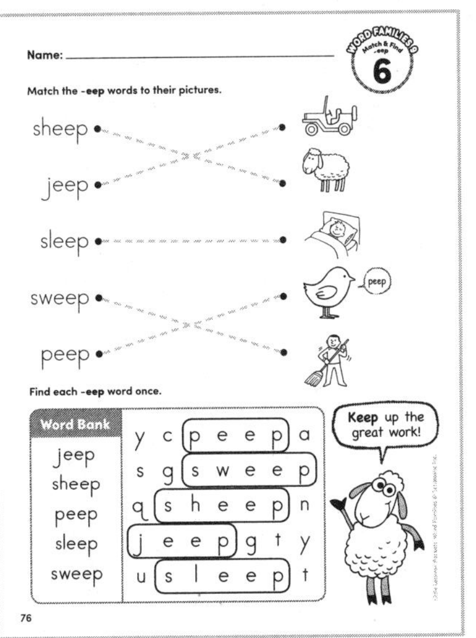
Name:
Word Families Match & Find -eep 6
Match the -eep words to their pictures.
sheep
jeep
sleep
sweep
peep
peep
Find each -eep word once.
Word Bank: jeep, sheep, peep, sleep, sweep

y	c	p	e	e	p	a
s	g	s	w	e	e	p
q	s	h	e	e	p	n
j	e	e	p	g	t	y
u	s	l	e	e	p	t

Keep up the great work!
76

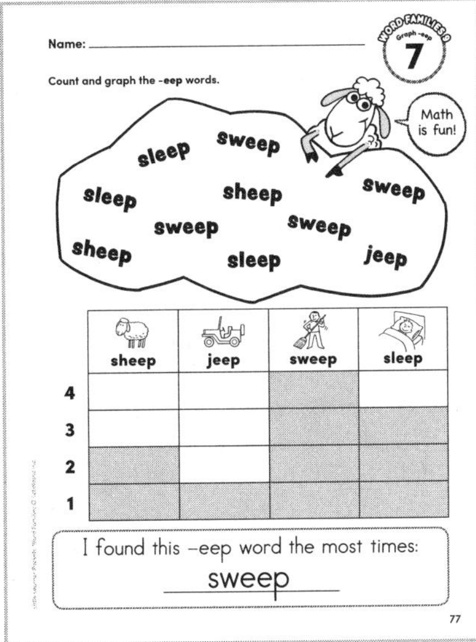
Name:
Word Families Graph -eep 7
Count and graph the -eep words.
sleep sweep sleep sheep sweep sweep sweep sheep sleep jeep
Math is fun!

	sheep	jeep	sweep	sleep
4				
3				
2				
1				

I found this -eep word the most times: sweep
77

Name:
Word Families Review -ee & -eep 8
Use each -ee and -eep word once to complete the story. Then read it aloud.

-ee	-eep
see	beep
bee	sheep
three	jeep

Bee and Sheep
See the striped bee!
See the white sheep!
They are in a jeep.
They see two birds and three big bears.
Beep, beep!
Great work! Bye!
78

PACKET 10
WORD FAMILIES
-ice, -ight

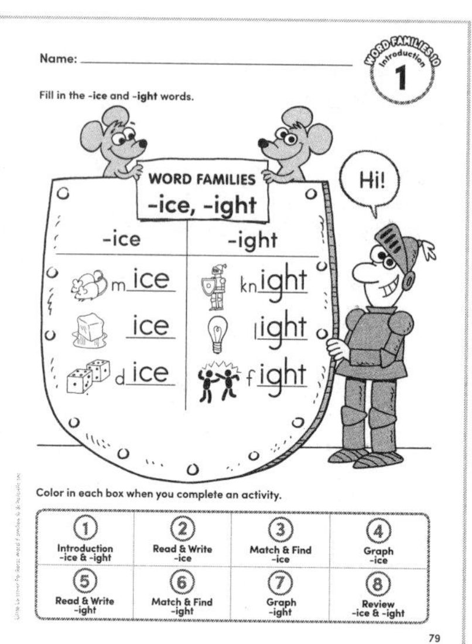
Name:
Fill in the -ice and -ight words.
WORD FAMILIES -ice, -ight
Hi!

-ice	-ight
mice	knight
ice	light
dice	fight

Color in each box when you complete an activity.

① Introduction -ice & -ight	② Read & Write -ice	③ Match & Find -ice	④ Graph -ice
⑤ Read & Write -ight	⑥ Match & Find -ight	⑦ Graph -ight	⑧ Review -ice & -ight

79

Name:
Read the sentence. Then write the words.
The nice mice eat a bowl of ice cream.
nice nice nice nice nice
mice mice mice mice
ice ice ice ice ice ice
Use the letters from the letter bank to make more -ice words.
Letter Bank: r, d, sl
sl ice — d ice — r ice
80

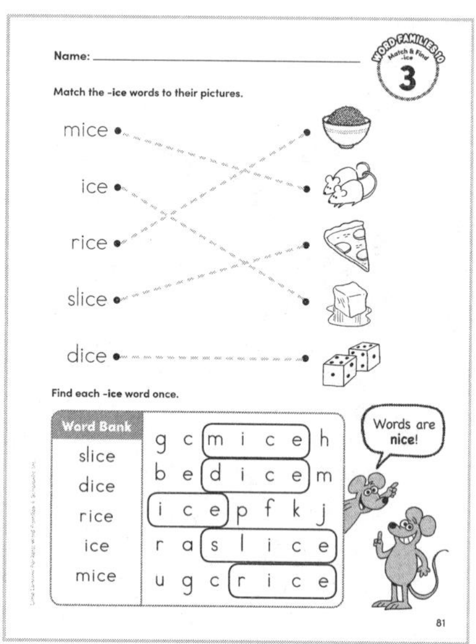
Name:
Match the -ice words to their pictures.
mice, ice, rice, slice, dice
Find each -ice word once.
Word Bank: slice, dice, rice, ice, mice
g c m i c e h
b e d i c e m
i c e p f k j
r a s l i c e
u g c r i c e
Words are nice!
81

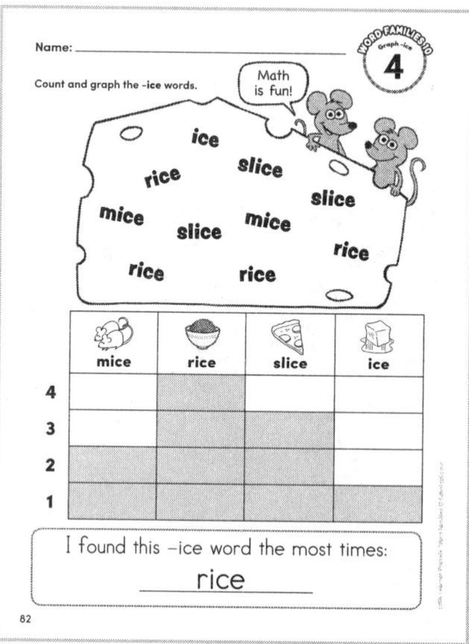
Name:
Count and graph the -ice words.
Math is fun!
ice, rice, slice, slice, mice, slice, mice, rice, rice, rice
mice | rice | slice | ice
4, 3, 2, 1
I found this -ice word the most times: rice
82

Name:
Read the sentence. Then write the words.
The knight saw a bright light in the sky.
knight knight knight
bright bright bright
light light light light
Use the letters from the letter bank to make more -ight words.
Letter Bank: n, fl, r
n ight — fl ight — r ight
83

Name:
Match the -ight words to their pictures.
knight, light, flight, fight, right
Find each -ight word once.
Word Bank: right, knight, fight, flight, light
f i g h t r a
f l i g h t d
q k r i g h t
r o l i g h t
k n i g h t z
You are right!
84

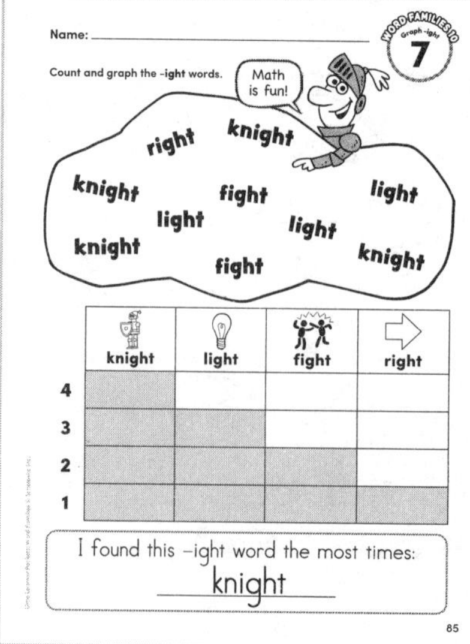
Name:
Count and graph the -ight words.
Math is fun!
right, knight, knight, fight, light, light, knight, light, fight, knight
knight | light | fight | right
4, 3, 2, 1
I found this -ight word the most times: knight
85

Name:
Use each -ice and -ight word once to complete the story. Then read it aloud.
Word Bank — -ice: slice, mice, nice; -ight: right, night, knight
The Mice and Knight
The mice are on the left.
The knight is on the right.
It is a starry night.
"Do you want a slice of pizza?" ask the two mice.
"Thank you," says the knight.
"That would be so nice!"
Great work! Bye!
86